P9-CDP-450

REV HUGH OCONNOR
2050 W BALL RD
ANAHEIM CA 92804

THE GLORY
OF ISRAEL

THE GLORY OF ISRAEL

scriptural background on
the mysteries of the rosary

by

Ronald Walls

Our Sunday Visitor, Inc.
Huntington, Indiana 46750

The Nihil Obstat and Imprimatur are official declarations that a book or pamphlet is free of doctrinal or moral error. No implication is contained therein that those who have granted the Nihil Obstat and Imprimatur agree with the contents, opinions or statements expressed.

Nihil Obstat:
REV. LAWRENCE GOLLNER
Censor Librorum

Imprimatur:
✝LEO A. PURSLEY, D.D.
Bishop of Fort Wayne-South Bend

ISBN: 0-87973-813-8

Library of Congress Catalog Card Number: 72-075088

Cover Design by James E. McIlrath

Published, printed and bound in the U.S.A. by
OUR SUNDAY VISITOR, INC.
Noll Plaza, Huntington, Indiana 46750

Contents

Acknowledgements

Quotation from St. Teresa of Avila is from *The Complete Works of St. Teresa,* translated and edited by E. Allison Peers from the critical edition of P. Silverio de Santa Teresa, D.C., published in three volumes by Sheed & Ward Inc., New York, and Sheed & Ward Ltd., London.

Excerpt from the Definition of Chalcedon is taken from *The Council of Chalcedon,* by R. V. Sellers, published by SPCK, London.

Quotations from the Dogmatic Constitution on the Church are reprinted with permission from *The Documents of Vatican II,* February 14, 1966. All rights reserved. C 1966. America Press, Inc., 106 West 56th Street, New York, N.Y. 10019. Published in the United Kingdom by Geoffrey Chapman.

Photos from Father Patrick Peyton's Family Rosary Crusade production of "The Fifteen Mysteries of the Rosary."

Preface

This book provides a series of theological meditations or homilies upon the scripture texts that lie behind those episodes in the life of our Lord and of his mother which have come to be known as the mysteries of the Rosary. The word "Rosary" evokes the immediate image of a set of beads; but the beads exist for the sake of the prayers which are said upon them, and the prayers for the sake of the mysteries to which they direct our thoughts. These mysteries, when studied carefully and in relation to one another, are found to contain a very full exposition of the whole story of man's salvation.

In recent years the Rosary has suffered decline in popularity. One of the causes of this decline has undoubtedly been the careless way in which the prayer of the Rosary has been practised. We have allowed the Rosary, which is a fairly lengthy vocal prayer, too often to become a kind of prayer-wheel — an external religious action, the performance of which is felt more or less to guarantee the acquisition of a quota of grace. Reaction away from the Rosary is, therefore, part of a justifiable reaction against mechanical prayer and the over-materialized concept of grace to which it is allied. Today there is a growing appreciation of grace as not so much a *thing* to be acquired in measurable quantity as a *quality* of soul, which develops by the gift of God, along with our deeper penetration of the mysteries of the Faith.

Paradoxically, the prayer of the Rosary, as meditation

upon episodes of the gospel, is designed precisely to advance this deeper penetration of the mystery of the Faith; is designed, that is, as a most true and effective means of acquiring grace, conceived in anything but a materialized way. To achieve its purpose, however, the Rosary must become true vocal prayer — prayer that is vocal and meditative at the same time. St. Teresa of Avila, the most recently acclaimed doctor of the Church, has some clear, common-sense comment to make on this very point.

". . . We may, of course, consider it enough to say our prayers as a mere habit, repeating the words and thinking that this will suffice. Whether it suffices or not I will not now discuss. Learned men must decide: . . . But what I should like, daughters, is for us not to be satisfied with that alone: when I say the Creed, it seems to me right, and indeed obligatory, that I should understand and know what it is that I believe; and when I repeat the 'Our Father,' my love should make me want to understand who this Father of ours is and who the Master is that taught us this prayer. . . .

"You will say at once that this is meditation, and that you are not capable of it, and do not even wish to practise it, but are content with vocal prayer. . . . You are right to say that what we have described is mental prayer; but I assure you that I cannot distinguish it from vocal prayer faithfully recited with a realization of who it is that we are addressing." (*The Way of Perfection,* chapter 24.)

If this is true of vocal prayer in general, it is doubly true of the Rosary in particular, for in the Rosary we are supposed to stretch our minds beyond the words of our prayer to the episodes in the life of our Lord and of his mother that we commemorate. Again we may turn to St. Teresa of Avila for helpful comment on meditative prayer.

". . . By meditation I mean prolonged reasoning with the understanding, in this way. We begin by thinking of the favor which God bestowed upon us by giving us His only Son; and we do not stop there but proceed to consider the mysteries of His whole glorious life. Or we begin with the prayer in the garden and go on rehearsing the events that follow until we come to the crucifixion. Or we take one episode of the passion — Christ's arrest, let us say — and go over this mystery in our mind, meditating in detail upon the points in it which we need to think over and try to realize, such as the treason of Judas, the flight of the apostles, and so on. This is an admirable and a most meritorious kind of prayer." (*The Interior Castle,* Mansions 6, chapter 7.)

Although St. Teresa does not explicitly mention the Rosary, this quotation gives us a hint not only of the method, but of the subject matter of Rosary meditation. Note St. Teresa's significant phrasing: "We begin by thinking etc. . . . and we do not stop there. . . . Or we begin with etc. . . . and go on . . . until . . ." The subject of our meditation is the whole, continuous story of man's salvation.

So often in the past, even when time has been taken to meditate upon the mysteries, people have failed to achieve their desired result because they have isolated the episodes and destroyed the continuity of the story. In this way the mysteries have become static tableaux and not incidents in a living drama. The truth is that the separate scenes in isolation are like a set of still frames such as we might see displayed outside a cinema. They give us a hint of the story; but we will not be satisfied until we have stepped inside and watched the whole drama unfolding before our eyes. Only then do the characters come alive. Otherwise they remain at the flat level of lifeless, painted images.

Fortunately for us we have the means to witness this great drama, for we have been plentifully provided with the script. In the Bible we have a set of books which introduce us to the characters in the great drama of man's salvation, and tell us what these characters are really saying. Adequate meditation upon the mysteries of the Rosary — that "prolonged reasoning with the understanding" of which St. Teresa speaks — turns out to be most perfectly supplied by study of the Bible; and because this is so, the prayer of the Rosary turns out to be very much in tune with the present-day insistence on the Bible as our chief source-book both of theology and of devotion.

This book attempts to supply a set of Bible-readings to match each mystery of the Rosary. The homily is designed as an exposition of these readings. The meditation thus provided is strictly biblical. That is to say, the New Testament incident associated directly with the mystery is interpreted through the mind of the Bible, as cherished by the Church. We try, therefore, not merely to stimulate our devout imagination by the New Testament scene, but to find out what the characters in that scene themselves felt about it. Thus, for example, in the Annunciation we try to discover exactly what must have been going on in our Lady's mind at the time. That is why we have dug so much into the Old Testament. This method of searching for the meaning of the mysteries also explains why the New Testament account of the mystery has been held over until after the homily. By the time we come to read the principal New Testament passage our minds are already prepared to adore the truth it contains. The reader need not, however, be bound by this arrangement in his use of the book. The meditations are presented in such a way that the worshipper may use as much or as little of each as he pleases at a time. He might read a single passage from the Old Testament, or all of the Bible passages, or just the homily. A priest might find the material of use as the basis for a public Bible-service. The object of the exercise is always to gain a deeper understanding of the story of man's salvation. This is the meat which will nourish our souls through this devotion. The number of "Rosaries" in the plural that we can recite is of minor importance.

Part One

THE JOYFUL
MYSTERIES

The Annunciation

Homily

The first page of the Bible declares the mystery of mysteries: God, infinite and self-sufficient, has broken the silence of his own eternity and spoken, thus creating a vast and splendid universe, including man, made in his own image. Then comes the story of man's sin. Through pride man exchanged original righteousness for original sin; the world ceased to be a paradise and became a vale of tears. But a glimmer of hope remained: from among the human race would come one who would bruise the serpent's head, that is break the power of the Devil. And so the vale of tears became a place of testing, of spiritual growth, and of hope. From the twelfth chapter of Genesis onwards the Bible tells the story of the re-creation of man, through God's calling the children of Israel to be his own special people.

When the angel Gabriel came and spoke to Mary, the story of man's re-creation was already in its very last chapter. And so, to understand this late incident we must cast our minds back across the history of the chosen people of whom our Lady was the final, perfect flowering. She herself would do this in order to fit this present incident into the whole sequence of events which made up God's dealing with her people down the centuries. Only thus could she understand the mysterious interview and assess its authenticity.

In fitting herself, as a humble servant of the Lord into the context of the history of his servant people of Israel, Mary would certainly recall Abraham, the great progenitor of her race. The angel himself guided her mind by telling her about her cousin Elizabeth, who found herself in exactly the same situation as Abraham's wife, Sarah. Abraham had obeyed God's call to leave a settled way of life in the prosperous, civilized society of Lower Mesopotamia and accept the life of a nomad. In addition he had believed God's promise that he would become the father of a mighty nation, although, humanly speaking, that was impossible. Thus Abraham set the pattern for all time of true religion. He became father of the faithful, the friend of God; and St. Paul, writing eighteen centuries later to the Christians of Rome, still harks back to Abraham: "Abraham is our father in the eyes of God, in whom he put his faith, and who brings the dead to life and calls into being what does not exist."

One of the chief proofs, in our Lady's eyes, that the angel's message came from God and not from Satan, was that it followed the same pattern as the message received by Abraham. There was a call to put herself completely at God's disposal, followed by a promise that seemed impossible of fulfillment in the natural course of events: she, although a virgin, would conceive and bear a son who, as Israel's Messiah, would bring a great blessing to all the nations of the earth. In the true tradition of Abraham, Mary obeyed the divine call and believed the promise.

Even so, the Gospel tells us, she was afraid; and, strangely enough, it was the angel's initial, apparently cheerful greeting that startled her. "Rejoice, so highly favoured! The Lord is with you" the angel said — a phrase that is echoed in the later greeting by Elizabeth who addressed her cousin thus: "Of all women you are the most blessed. . . ." Something about these very words seems to have frightened our Lady.

Our Lady was startled because again she was recalling parts of the story of her people. This time we find the clue in the story of Judith — a Hollywood script if ever there was. No wonder our Lady was startled when she received this hint of the type of role she was being asked to fill. The main part of the story is contained in Judith, chapters 10-13.

The tiny Jewish nation, faithful witness to the one true and holy God, was besieged by the mighty army of Holofernes, whose ambition was to bring the whole world into idolatrous subjection to Nebuchadnezzar. When the situation seemed utterly hopeless, the widow Judith, renowned for her prayer and ritual purity, set her bold plan in motion. By a ruse she gained entrance to Holofernes' camp, while assuring herself of free passage out again. On the fourth night of her stay in the camp Holofernes gave a banquet and ordered his personal servant: "Go and persuade that Hebrew woman you are looking after to come and join us and eat and drink in our company. We shall be disgraced if we let a woman like this go without knowing her better. If we do not seduce her, everyone will laugh at us!" Judith accepted the invitation, but sat on her own rug and ate and drank the provisions she had brought with her, to avoid ritual impurity. Holofernes became so excited that he drank far more than he had ever drunk before. Finally the servant got everyone out of the room, leaving Holofernes alone with Judith. By this time, however, Holofernes had collapsed in a stupor. With a prayer for strength, Judith took down the scymitar from the bedpost and hacked off Holofernes' head. She hid the head in her food basket and hurried off, as she had done on the three previous nights, as if to pray outside the camp. Soon the Israelites were rejoicing as the head of their mighty adversary was displayed to them, and Judith was acclaimed in these words:

> "May you be blessed, my daughter, by God Most High, beyond all women on earth.

> "You are the glory of Jerusalem!

You are the pride of Israel!
You are the highest honour of our race!

"By doing all this with your own hand
you have deserved well of Israel,
and God has approved what you have done.

"May you be blessed by the Lord Almighty
in all the days to come!"

Now this story is more of an allegory than a piece of history. In some ways this is what makes it so significant. It has a spiritual meaning which was applied to our Lady by the angel Gabriel, and is commended to us by St. Luke, so that we may understand who our Lady really is. She is Judith, the perfect Jewess who lives by prayer and is completely pure — the ritual purity of the Old Testament being the symbol of the spiritual and moral purity of our Lady —; she is the one who "with her own hand" — that is by her free choice — has "deserved well of Israel," and earned the title of blessed "in all the days to come"; she is the long-awaited seed of the first Eve, and has crushed the serpent's head — symbolized by the spectacular action of Judith in hacking off the head of Holofernes.

And so the ancient promise of Genesis has been fulfilled: our Lady is the second Eve who, completely immaculate of soul, has listened to the voice of God — not that of the serpent — and has obeyed, thus reversing the situation brought about by the first Eve. Mary has brought forth the Savior of the world: she is the mother of God and mother, too, of the new chosen people, all Christ's brethren. Her posterity, like that of Abraham, is as the sands of the seashore in number, and all generations call her blessed.

Gospel: Luke 1:26-38

The Visitation

Bible-readings

Exodus 24:16-18	The glory of God on Sinai
Exodus 40:34-38	The Cloud and the Fire
2 Samuel 6:2-15	The ark of the Covenant
1 Kings 8:1-6; 10-13	The ark is brought to the Temple
Zephaniah 3:14-18	Psalms of joy in Zion
Ecclesiasticus 24:1-22	The Wisdom of God

Homily

The long training of the descendants of Abraham had at last produced the desired result. In Mary this race had produced one who, like Eve before the Fall, was quite unspoiled by the universal sin of mankind. As in the Graden of Eden, so now at Nazareth as the angel addressed Mary, human destiny hung in the balance. Would the Second Eve use her perfect freedom of will as the First Eve had done, to resist the word of God, or would she, by love and obedience, open up the way for the Redeemer of mankind to come and save the human race? With our Lady's, "Let what you have said be done to me," we reach a critical point in the story of salvation. A fresh start had been made in the name of all mankind. But, as Mary herself knew, this was only the start of the final phase in the story of salvation. Battle had been joined with Satan, but final victory was not yet won; the Serpent's head had been bruised, the Devil was dazed and dumbfounded, but not yet totally vanquished. As the First Eve

paved the way for Adam's fall, so the Second Eve, by her indispensable cooperation with God, had paved the way for the advent of the Second Adam, the Lord from heaven; and it is towards this mysterious and magnificent figure that our minds have already been turned in the story of the Annunciation. The Child whom Mary is to bear is announced as the mighty king of Israel, the Son of the Most High; and he is to be named Jesus, which means "Savior."

To clarify her mind even more about who exactly her child was to be, at the hint from the angel, Mary set off to consult her cousin Elizabeth, who, like her, was to bear a son in extraordinary circumstances. As she travelled towards the hills of Judaea — for her cousin's home was at Ain Karim, about five miles west of Jerusalem — her mind began to pick up another thread in her people's tradition.

The thought had been started up by the angel's words, "The power of the Most High will cover you with its shadow." The angel had used words which referred directly to the cloud in which the Israelites of old had seen God's presence upon earth. At mount Sinai, when Moses received the Law, the glory of God had appeared in a cloud, which seemed like a devouring fire. On coming down from the mountain, Moses had built a tent according to the pattern revealed to him. This tent was to serve as a meeting place for the people, and as a sanctuary for their God.

The ark of the Covenant was the most precious piece of furniture in this tent, and the cloud of God's presence — the Shekinah as it was called — settled above the ark. When God wished the people to move on in the wilderness, the Shekinah rose from the ark, and the people were led on their journey by a cloud by day and a pillar of fire by night. At a later date King David brought the ark up from the west to his own citadel of Zion, but the ark rested for three months at the home of Obed-edom. Finally, King Solomon built a temple in Jerusalem to house the ark and the presence of God. In later Jewish tradition the Shekinah came to be identified with the Wisdom of God, conceived almost as a second divine Person.

With the collapse of the kingdom of Judah and the destruction of the Temple by the Babylonians in 589 B.C., the glory of

God seemed to have departed from Israel. The Temple was desecrated, the people taken off into captivity. The faith of Israel, however, not only remained, but was purified and strengthened. When the captives — or rather their offspring — returned home some seventy years later they set about rebuilding the Temple and reconstituting their national and religious life under the leadership of Ezra and Nehemiah.

Now the veneration of God's presence in their midst began to take on a fresh character. The devout among the Jews seemed to sense that the Lord would come to dwell with his people in an even more significant way than he had done in the cloud above the ark of the Covenant. The Temple and its worship was already becoming, in their eyes, more of a symbol than a reality. The devout who waited for the consolation of Israel were thinking more and more of the Messiah, the wonderful Savior who was to come and redeem his people, as the prophets had foretold. His return would be the true return of the glory of God to Israel. This new and expectant mentality is expressed, for example, by the prophet Zephaniah:

"Shout for joy, daughter of Zion,
Israel, shout aloud! . . .
Yahweh, the king of Israel, is in your midst;
you have no more evil to fear."

Our Lady was steeped in the traditional belief in the presence of God in the Shekinah, and she was born into an atmosphere of expectancy of the final Messianic coming of God to his people. As she journeyed towards her cousin's home, the whole picture became clearer to her. The angel, she realized, had compared *her* to the ark of the Covenant, the bearer of the Shekinah. He was telling her that she was to be the mother of the Wisdom of God. And now, as her journey progressed, this thought received dramatic confirmation: was she not travelling through the hill country of Judaea, just as the ark of the Covenant had done at King David's command? And, as on that memorable journey of old, she, too, the living and more perfect ark, did not go directly to Jerusalem, but made a halt on the way. Thus Mary came to the home of her cousin Elizabeth.

It was here, in the happy atmosphere of family and of a shared faith, that Mary received further confirmation that she was the new ark of the Covenant, the bearer of no less than God's own presence upon earth. No sooner had Mary greeted her cousin than the babe in Elizabeth's womb leapt, just as David had leapt and danced before the ark of the Covenant; and Elizabeth, inspired by God, repeated anew the substance of the angel's greeting to Mary, adding these words: "Why should I be honored with a visit from the mother of my Lord?" — words that are a direct parallel to those spoken by King David: "However can the ark of Yahweh come to me?" St. Luke carries the parallelism even further in his postscript: "Mary stayed with Elizabeth about three months . . ." — the length of time that the ark of Yahweh had stayed with the family of Obed-edom.

And so, our Lady learned that this Messiah, the Savior of Israel, was mysteriously identical with the presence, the glory, the Wisdom, of God, and she was to be his mother. The prophecy that is recorded on the very last page of the Old Testament was being fulfilled: "Look, I am going to send my messenger to prepare a way before me. And the Lord you are seeking will suddenly enter his Temple; and the angel of the covenant (i.e. God himself) whom you are longing for, yes, he is coming, says Yahweh Sabaoth. Who will be able to resist the day of his coming? Who will remain standing when he appears?" (Malachi 3:1-2)

Gospel: Luke 1:39-45; 56

The Nativity

Homily

At Christmas time we love to sing hymns and carols in which the shepherds and their flocks figure prominently. But do we realize that this pastoral setting, which forms the background to the story of the manifestation of the Word made flesh in the birth of Jesus, is much more than a bit of local, decorative color? St. Luke tells of the shepherds and their flocks for a specific theological reason. He is recalling that day at Bethlehem when David was called from minding his father's sheep, and was anointed by Samuel to be king of Israel. By mentioning Bethlehem, the shepherds, and Joseph — who was of David's line — St. Luke is declaring that God's promise, that David's dynasty would endure for ever, and that from this dynasty would come the Messiah-King, has been fulfilled. St. Matthew tells us that Jesus was born in Bethlehem, and quotes a prophecy from the book of Micah, which speaks of the leader who will be born here, and "who will shepherd my people Israel." In place of the

23

adoration of the shepherds, however, St. Matthew has the story of the visit of the three non-Jewish kings from the east. These men represent the whole human race, and reveal the fulfillment of another prophecy of Isaiah:

". . . the riches of the sea will flow to you,
the wealth of the nations come to you;
camels in throngs will cover you,
and dromedaries of Midian and Ephah;
everyone in Sheba will come,
bringing gold and incense
and singing the praise of Yahweh."

(Isaiah 60:5-6)

The story has been rounded off. The promise to Abraham has been fulfilled: all the nations of the earth have been blessed in his posterity; the promise to David has likewise been fulfilled: the Messiah-King has been born from his dynasty; and the Wisdom of God, who guided the Israelites through the wilderness into the Promised Land and came to rest in the Shekinah above the ark of the Covenant within the Holy of Holies in the Temple has finally descended to earth to become flesh and blood in the womb of the virgin Mary, and be born a child in the crib at Bethlehem. All the strands of Old Testament expectation converge in the Babe of Bethlehem, and we come to the fundamental mystery of the Christian faith, a mystery which Isaiah glimpsed long before when he gave the Messiah the supreme title of Immanual — "God with us" — , a mystery the importance of which we acknowledge when we bow our heads as we recite these words in the Creed: ". . . was incarnate of the virgin Mary by the power of the Holy Spirit, and was made man."

Our Lady, we are told by St. Luke, stored up in her heart all of these episodes in the drama of salvation as they followed one another in mysterious sequence. This event, however, the birth of her son, must have been for her, as it is for us, the deepest mystery of all. Our Lady, as no one else could ever be, was aware of the paradox, that here was one who was both God and man. The angel had told her that the child born to her would be the Son of the Most High, and had alluded to the Shekinah above the ark of the Covenant so that she would know that he meant what he said. And she believed the angel. As Elizabeth commented: "Blessed is she who believed that the promise made to her by the Lord would be fulfilled." At the same time she knew, as no one else ever could, that he was truly her baby, her flesh and blood.

The New Testament writers take up this same theme in the way they present the story of our Lord's life. The evangelists are at pains to declare that Jesus is Lord, that is no less than God himself. St. John puts it quite explicitly when he reports our Lord's saying: "The Father and I are one" and "Before Abraham ever was, I am." The miracles, too, are not just impressive wonders but signs of our Lord's divinity, miracles which symbolized the giving of life — something which pertains to God alone; and he often performed the miracle on the Sabbath, precisely because that was the day consecrated to God alone. As he said when challenged: "My Father works on this day, and so do I." In association with another miracle, he pointed out that he did it to demonstrate that he had power to forgive sins — again the prerogative of God. Calming a storm likewise was considered an activity specially reserved to the power of the Creator.

But this open declaration of our Lord's divinity by the evangelists never causes them to obscure his humanity. The Gospels present a picture of a real man who ate and slept and even wept. And at the end his humanity is all too convincingly revealed in his slow and agonized death.

There can be no doubt at all that the New Testament tells us plainly that Jesus Christ is true God and true man.

The doctrinal history of the Church in the first few centuries is the story of how the faithful fought to maintain the integrity of this mystery. In an attempt to release the tension of this paradox and reduce the mystery to terms comprehensible to the mind of man, now one side and now the other was denied. Some said that Jesus was the Son of God only in a metaphorical sense, that he merely had some kind of perfect relationship with God. Others, again, said that he was truly God, but that his manhood was merely a disguise; that he made use of the appearance of a human body, but was not fully man. In face of these errors from two opposite directions, the Church always maintained the basic truth that mankind could only be redeemed by one who was truly God, and, on the other hand, that anything in our human nature that had not been assumed by the Word of God could not have been redeemed. The Church was never able to explain this mystery, but resolutely preserved it intact, thus handing on for all generations the initial experience of our Lady when first she beheld her own child, who was, none the less, the Son of God as well.

It is interesting and helpful for us to read part of the statement made by the fourth ecumenical council of the Church — a council which met at Chalcedon in the year 451. This council defined how we should speak about our Lord Jesus Christ so as to deny neither his divinity nor his humanity. The statement is not an *explanation* of the mystery; it merely keeps us on the right track along which we can travel to a deeper contemplation of the truth and so find nourishment for our souls.

"Our Lord Jesus Christ is one and the same Son, the same perfect in Godhead, the same perfect in manhood, truly God and truly man, . . . one and the same Christ, Son, Lord, only-begotten, made known in two natures (which exist) without confusion, without change, without division, without separation; the difference of the natures having been in no wise taken away by reason of the union, but rather the properties of each nature being preserved, and both concurring into one person. . . ."

In making this dogmatic statement, the Fathers of Chalcedon were simply expanding what St. Paul had said in essence in the very opening verses of his letter to the Romans: "This news is about the Son of God who, according to the human nature he took, was a descendant of David: it is about Jesus Christ our Lord who, in the order of the spirit, the spirit of holiness that was in him, was proclaimed Son of God in all his power through his resurrection from the dead."

Gospel: John 1:1-14

The Presentation
in the Temple

Daniel 9:20-24	The anointing of the Temple
Luke 1:5-25	Zechariah's vision
Exodus 13:11-16	The redemption of the first-born
Malachi 3:1-4	The Lord will come to his Temple
Isaiah 49:1-6	The Light of the Nations
Psalm 48:9-14	Zion, the mountain of God

Homily

The passage cited above from the book of Daniel supplies a background to the story in St. Luke's Gospel of the vision of Zechariah, father of John the Baptist. In both scenes a prophetic soul is at prayer at the hour of the evening sacrifice, when the angel Gabriel appears to him, bringing a message from God. The purpose of this literary background would seem to be to indicate the time sequence of the infancy narrative in St. Luke's Gospel. St. Luke is drawing attention to the six months of Elizabeth's pregnancy plus the nine months of our Lady's pregnancy plus the forty days until the Purification, the sum of which is seventy weeks of days — the time that was to pass between the moment of Daniel's vision and the anointing of the Holy of Holies. This is St. Luke's way of impressing upon his readers the profound theological significance of the Presentation of Jesus in the Temple. This event was the true coming of the Lord to his

Temple, the authentic anointing of the Holy of Holies, the final return of the glory of God, of the Shekinah, to Zion.

The story of Zechariah's vision, which has the same framework as the vision of Daniel concerning the anointing of the Temple, introduces the figure of John the Baptist. This is another important feature in the narrative of our Lord's infancy. The emergence of a prophetic forerunner was regarded as one of the signs authenticating the coming of the Messiah, and, so St. Luke tells us, the forerunner has come. The oracle of Malachi, which links the expectation of the forerunner with that of the Lord coming suddenly to his Temple, has been fulfilled.

The whole literary background to the story of the Presentation thus stresses the point that has been the preoccupation of the Gospel story so far: the mystery of our Lord's person and nature, and, incidentally, our Lady's unique place in the divine scheme of salvation. With the story of the Presentation in the Temple at Jerusalem we begin to sense the introduction of a new element, the element of action, the hint of the means whereby this Lord of the Temple is going to accomplish the salvation which it is his office to bring to his people.

This new element appears with the report of how Mary and Joseph faithfully carried out all the prescriptions of the Law concerning the birth of a first-born son. First of all, eight days after his birth, they had had the child circumcised. A mere drop of the infant's blood was shed, and by this symbolic act he was shown to be truly of the seed of Abraham, and, implicitly, true man. Then, in the Presentation scene, forty days after the birth, our Lady came to the Temple for the ceremony of her purification and offered the sacrifice of the poor — a pair of turtle doves and two young pigeons. But whereas St. Luke explicitly tells how the purificatory sacrifice as specified in Leviticus 12:8 was offered, he is silent about the payment of the redemption-price for the first-born son (Num. 18:15-16). This silence is eloquent. How inappropriate it would have been to pay a redemption-price to the Temple on behalf of him who was Lord of the Temple! This silence underlines yet again the fact that here is God himself now coming to claim possession of his Temple.

But the deep truth behind this silence is not thereby exhausted. There is another, more poignant reason for exemption from payment of the ritual redemption-price. This child alone among all of the first-born males of his people would not be exempt from paying the real price of which this ransom-money was a mere symbol. Resembling rather the first-born of the flock, whose actual sacrifice was required, he, too, would have to go through with the grim reality of sacrificial slaughter. The Servant of the Lord of whom Isaiah sang, was to be not only a light to enlighten every nation, but a suffering servant. The anointing of the Holy of Holies would be performed in the blood of him who was no less than Lord of the Temple.

Finally this theme of sacrifice is taken up quite explicitly — although in deep sayings — by the prophet Simeon, with whose oracle the account of the Presentation ends. Simeon looks upon the child, and, first, takes up the strain of Isaiah's prophecy, hailing the child as the glory of Israel and the light of all nations. Then, turning to Mary, he proclaims that her child will lead to a crisis among his people: some will see him and believe; others will look upon him with blind eyes and reject him, thus pronouncing judgment upon themselves. Simeon's brief comment reminds us of our Lord's own sayings as recorded by St. John:

> "On these grounds is sentence pronounced:
> that though the light has come into the world
> men have shown they prefer
> darkness to light
> because their deeds were evil." (John 3:19)

> "It is for judgment
> that I have come into this world,
> so that those without sight may see
> and those with sight turn blind." (John 9:39)

And so the prophet Simeon, speaking of the rejection of Christ, picks up the theme of sacrifice adumbrated in the symbolism of the non-payment of the redemption-price. He foretells, therefore, the ultimate rejection of this child, of his meek acceptance of his role as sacrificial lamb upon the cross.

Simeon's last word is addressed to Mary. Here, as so often, there are subtle overtones from the Old Testament which give us a clue to the meaning of what is being said. In the second servant song of Isaiah, which contains the reference to the "light of the nations," there is this phrase also:

"Yahweh called me before I was born,
from my mother's womb he pronounced my name.
He made my mouth a sharp sword,
and hid me in the shadow of his hand."

Was Simeon's mind perhaps fastening upon this imagery and thinking of the child, whose very nature and function was to precipitate crisis, as though he were cutting into the very being of his own mother? Whatever the explanation of the sequence of thoughts in Simeon's mind — and certainly his mind as a prophet was the product of Old Testament prophecy — his saying becomes most meaningful when we relate it to the sacrificial scene of Calvary which is the general background to the whole incident. There, Jesus' mother, beholding her Son, must have felt his agony in her own soul. Moreover, in her deep union with her Son she stood at the foot of the cross as representative of the whole Church. We, too, are supposed to enter into his sufferings, to "make up what is lacking in the sufferings of Christ, for the sake of his body, which is the Church." Thus in her union with the passion of her Son she revealed what would come about in the hearts of all the faithful down the ages.

Gospel: Luke 2:21-40

The Finding
in the Temple

Bible-readings

Deuteronomy 16:1-8	The Passover
1 Samuel 1:19-28	Samuel's vocation
Isaiah 6:1-13	The glory of God fills the Temple
Proverbs 3:13-26	Full of Wisdom
Hebrews 10:1-18	The offering of his body
John 4:21-24	True worshippers

Homily

The first section of St. Luke's Gospel ends with an account of
that phase in our Lord's life when he is passing from childhood
to the acceptance of adult responsibility in the Jewish communi-
ty. For the young Jew this transition took place at the age of
twelve, and was marked by his first attendance at the feast of the
Passover in Jerusalem. As in the previous scene, therefore, sacrifice again is the background theme, for the Passover was the
great sacrificial feast of the Jews.

Central to this feast was the sacrifice of the Paschal Lamb.
In origin this rite was connected with the sacrifice of the first-
fruits of the flock — the significance of which we noted in our
meditation upon the Presentation in the Temple. This sacrifice,
however, had come to be attached to the decisive national historical event, the deliverance out of Egypt. The Passover was
thus primarily the commemoration of the salvation of the people of Israel. The second part of the Passover feast likewise was

a commemoration of that same event, when the Israelites had eaten a hasty meal of unleavened bread as they were about to escape out of Egypt.

In this scene our Lord is accepting his vocation as an adult Jew. In the eyes of St. Luke he is presenting himself in the Temple as the new Paschal Lamb, by whose sacrifice, not only the Jews, but the whole human race is to be redeemed. And we see also a foreshadowing of the new Passover meal which, in due course, he will institute as a memorial and representation of this redemptive sacrifice.

Commenting upon Exodus 12:1-20, which describes the Jewish Passover, the *Jerusalem Bible* has a most instructive footnote: "The Jewish Passover hence becomes a rehearsal for the Christian Passover: the Lamb of God, Christ, is sacrificed (the cross) and eaten (the Last Supper) within the framework of the Jewish Passover (the first Holy Week). Thus he brings salvation to the world; and the mystical re-enactment of this redemptive act becomes the central feature of the Christian liturgy, organized round the Mass which is at once sacrifice and sacrificial meal."

The presence of Jesus in the Temple, as an infant and again when he was twelve years old, sets him in relation not only to the Passover, but to the Day of Atonement and to the whole system of Temple worship. The sacrifices of the Temple had been a means of preparing men for the perfect worship that Christ would inaugurate. With his coming these had served their purpose, and were to be superseded by the offering of the body of Christ. Chapters 7 to 10 of the Letter to the Hebrews contains a dissertation on the perfect sacrifice of Christ. There we read that "He is abolishing the first sort (of sacrifice) to replace it with the second. . ." And the purpose of this is "for us to be made holy by the offering of his body made once and for all in Jesus Christ." In this new order of worship Christ is everything: victim, high-priest, the Temple of God in this world. As our great high-priest he has entered into the heavenly temple and leads us right into the presence of our eternal Father.

The Presentation and the Finding of Jesus in the Temple thus link up with other passages in the New Testament where the Temple is mentioned. There is the occasion when Jesus drove the money-changers out of the Temple, thereby declaring the inadequacy of the Jewish ritual, when he justified his action by saying, "Destroy this sanctuary, and in three days I will raise it up." By this he meant that the temple of his body would supply what the Jewish Temple could not, viz., a way of communication with God the Father of all mankind. And there is the very important incident at the well of Sychar when Jesus told the Samaritan woman that the day was coming when men would worship God neither upon mount Gerizim nor upon mount Zion, but in Spirit and in truth, that is in him who is the new mount Zion, the new Jerusalem, the new Temple.

It is against the background of Jesus as the true Temple that we must interpret the end of this scene, when Mary and Joseph, after three days searching, found Jesus talking with the teachers in the Temple. St. Luke is not trying to comment on the psychology or ethics of family life, is not describing an incident typical of parent-adolescent tension. He is continuing his teaching about the nature of Christ and his vocation. It is true, Jesus' immediate reply implies that his mother and foster-father had no real need to feel anxiety over him. But why? Because of who he was. His whole life was to be one of complete dedication to his Father. As the child Samuel had spent his whole life since babyhood away from his natural home in the service of the Temple, while his mother came up and down each year with clothing for him, so Jesus' normal place of residence was away from home, in his Father's house symbolized here by his remaining while his mother set off again back home; but, as his subsequent return to Nazareth indicates, pursuit of his Father's affairs was not a matter of remaining in the Temple at Jerusalem either. The Wisdom of God dwelt fully in him, and, wherever he was, there he was busied about his Father's affairs. When Jesus asks: "Did you not know that I must be busy with my Father's affairs?" he is not trying to justify his action, but inviting his whole people, Israel, represented by Mary and Joseph, to ponder on who he is and what he has been called to do. In the question we might even detect a hint of his more anguished exclamation when he caught sight of Jerusalem and its Temple as he approached them for the last time: "If you in your turn had only understood this day the message of peace!"

This appeal of our Lord to his people for their understanding and faith points to the final element in the concept of Christ as the true Temple of God upon earth. This new Temple must be filled with worshippers. By God's presence on earth we mean primarily his Son, born of the virgin Mary, dying upon the cross and rising from the dead, continuing sacramentally in his eucharistic body and blood, by which he makes present his sacrifice day by day and feeds his people, who, in turn, through the Holy Spirit are built up into the real and ever-present temple of God upon earth. St. Paul says: "That is what we are — the temple of the living God" (2 Cor. 6:16). As in the pictures in the apses of ancient churches, the Good Shepherd never appears unless surrounded by his sheep. The ultimate mystery and joy of the presence of God with us is that — as in the vision of Isaiah — his train fills the temple. His holiness flows truly into us. Christ has "offered himself as the perfect sacrifice to God" so that "we can purify our inner self from dead actions so that we do our service to the living God." His sacrifice has been effective as the sacrifices under the old covenant could never be. "By virtue of that one single offering he has achieved the eternal perfection of all whom he is sanctifying." And so God's people join in the declaration from Psalm 40, put by the writer of the Letter to the Hebrews into the mouth of Christ: "You who wanted no sacrifices or oblation, prepared a body for me. You took no pleasure in holocausts or sacrifices for sin; then I said . . . 'God, here I am! I am coming to obey your will.'"

Gospel: Luke 2:41-52

Part Two

THE SORROWFUL
MYSTERIES

The Agony in the Garden

Bible-readings

Zechariah 13:7-9	The sheep scattered
Hebrews 7:1-19	A priest for ever
Romans 7:14-25	The inward struggle
Matthew 17:1-8	The Transfiguration
Luke 22:39-62	The beginning of the Passion
John 12:23-28	"Now my soul is troubled"

Homily

The five joyful mysteries of the Rosary, based upon the first two chapters of St. Luke's Gospel, have provided us with very much more than a superficial historical record of our Lord's birth and growing up. They have turned out to contain a profound theological statement about who our Lord really is, an adumbration of his atoning sacrifice, and even a glimpse of his victory and enduring presence on earth in his new people. The infancy narrative and the Rosary mysteries based upon it are, indeed, a poetic statement of the whole framework of the story of salvation, with special emphasis laid not upon our Lord's humanity, as we might have expected in an infancy story, but upon the mystery of his divinity. Having thus firmly established our Lord's identity, and heralded his coming sacrifice, the Bible and the mysteries of the Rosary go on to spell out the details of that sacrifice as it was agonizingly offered by Christ in his human nature.

The quotation from Hebrews, with which we closed our

meditation on the fifth joyful mystery, forms a natural transition to the first sorrowful mystery, in which we begin to meditate more particularly upon our Lord's humanity: "You prepared a body for me . . . I said 'God, here I am! I am coming to obey your will' "; for the central theme of this mystery is the agonizing conflict between the spirit and the flesh, between knowledge of God's will and the body's powerful natural instinct for self-preservation, and how, in this conflict, Jesus overcame the frailty inherent in his humanity and, with a perfect heart, sacrificed his body for the sake of God's will.

In recounting this incident, St. Luke, who in his infancy story had been at pains to use all his poetic and theological talent to stress the divinity of Christ, takes trouble now to stress the reality of Christ's conflict and human agony. He of all the evangelists says that an angel came to give our Lord strength. That is, just as men cry out in such a trial for some supernatural assistance, so our Lord was human enough to have to cry out in like manner. And Luke also tells us that "his sweat fell to the ground like great drops of blood." In this way he underlines the reality of our Lord's agony.

The three evangelists, Matthew, Mark, and Luke, bring out the reality of the agony in another way. All link the scene with the foretelling of Peter's denial, when he, after thrice being put to the test, would persist in disclaiming all knowledge of Jesus; and all three include in the agony scene our Lord's admonition to the disciples to "Pray not to be put to the test." Our Lord is comparing his own testing here with the kind of testing that is bound to come upon his disciples. It is no less real a testing for him than it will be for them, and he too must resort to the only aid available — prayer to his heavenly Father. The evangelists are telling us that our Lord's divinity did not cause his testing to be less than that which men from time to time endure.

They suggest, indeed, that it was much more. Matthew and Mark say that Jesus took Peter and James and John aside with him to be witnesses of his agony, just as he had taken them to be witnesses of his transfiguration. The implied contrast between the two scenes suggests that as the former had been unspeakable in splendor so the latter was unutterable in horror. Being joined with divinity did not deprive our Lord's humanity of its natural sensitivity to suffering. The very opposite was true. The knowledge Christ had as God was what gave rise to the intensity of his agony. He knew exactly what was about to happen to him, and could fathom, as no man could ever fathom, the mysterious horror of being saddled with the sin of the whole world. He was about to go down and perform the spiritual equivalent of cleaning out a cesspool with his bare hands. In some sense, which baffles the mind of man, he was about to come so closely in contact with sin as to take upon himself the blame for all the ugliest and meanest things that have ever been done or ever will be done until the end of the world. As St. Paul puts it: "He was made sin for us" (2 Cor. 5:21). This was a horror that God alone could really appreciate, and this our Lord faced and accepted. And so, St. Luke tells us, when he returned from his agony, having decided to go through with all this, he found the disciples "sleeping from sheer grief." They had been unable to look on at his suffering.

Finding the disciples asleep, Jesus roused them with the words: "You can sleep on now and take your rest. It is all over" (Mk. 14:41). He had no further need of their spasmodic and unreliable prayers, for his victory was won. The words, "It is all over" remind us of Jesus' last words from the cross (Jn. 19:30): "It is accomplished." Perhaps the true climax of our Lord's passion was his agony in the garden. There, by reason of his divine foreknowledge, he endured all his physical sufferings in advance, along with the mental agony of his spiritual association with the sin of the world. The decision he then made to drink the cup of suffering offered him by his Father in heaven was his essential victory.

If we see our Lord's passion and victory over sin primarily in the interior submission of his will, which reached a climax in the agony in the garden, we find it easier to understand the relationship between the sacrifice once offered upon the cross and the sacrifice renewed all down the ages upon the altar in the celebration of the holy eucharist. Both cross and eucharist are external manifestations of an interior sacrifice of will, of the infinite and eternal mediation of Christ the high priest who has entered into the heavenly sanctuary, having first "offered himself as the perfect sacrifice to God through the eternal Spirit." The efficacy of the cross is presented eternally by the great high priest in the heavenly sanctuary; the Church joins her offering with that eternal presentation and so with the efficacy of the cross, every time she offers the bread and wine in the sacrifice of the Mass. Christ's sacrifice was unique — once for all — but there is a sense in which his sacrifice is perpetual. Christ's sacrifice, eternally presented before the Father in heaven, continually descends with power to earth — like great drops of blood falling to the ground.

Gospel: Mark 14:22-42

The Scourging at the Pillar

Homily

The scourging of our Lord forms the culmination of a sequence of events: his arrest in the garden, his trial before the Jewish court, and his trial before two secular courts. The scourging is the first act which manifests the judgment of the Son of God by men. Behind the horror of the action, therefore, is the appalling situation which made it possible: darkness is displacing light, justice is being utterly perverted, truth is being made to stand upon its head, man is imputing to One who is sinless, all those sins of which man himself is guilty. Man and God are changing places.

In the third chapter of his Gospel St. John reports our Lord's saying: "Everybody who does wrong hates the light and avoids it, for fear his actions should be exposed. . . ." The scene upon which we now meditate begins at the dead of night. Guided by Judas, the Temple guard set out under cover of darkness to arrest Jesus. To justify arresting Jesus, the Temple auth-

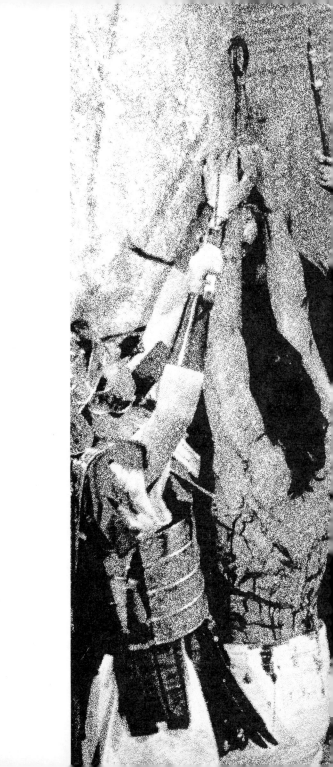

orities have to pretend that they are out to apprehend a danger-
ous political agitator, although in all his teaching, Jesus had in-
sisted that he had no political ambitions at all. This insistence
was summed up in his reply to Pilate: "Mine is not a kingdom of
this world; if my kingdom were of this world my men would
have fought to prevent my being surrendered to the Jews." And
so, as the guard approach to take him, Jesus reproves both the
absurdity and the hypocrisy of their action in the words: "Am I
a brigand that you had to set out with swords and clubs? When I
was among you in the Temple day after day you never moved to
lay hands on me. But this is your hour; this is the reign of darkness." The hypocrisy of Jesus' accusers reaches its climax when,
in response to Pilate's offer to release Jesus, they demand the
release of Barabbas, whose crime was the very one they pretend-
ed so zealously to abhor — insurrection against the Romans.

Before taking Jesus to the Roman court of justice, however,
where they brought this accusation of inciting the mob to revolt,
they took him to the supreme Jewish court, the Sanhedrin. In
this court false witnesses were procured in an attempt to convice
Jesus of blasphemy. This was another piece of quite unnecessary
perjury, for Jesus was perfectly willing quietly to admit to what
the authorities assumed was blasphemy. The high priest asked:
"Are you the Christ, the Son of the Blessed One?" Jesus answered simply: "I am" thus using the name of God himself.
Hearing this, the high priest tore his robes and shouted out:
"What need have we of witnesses now?" Their minds were made
up. He was to die, whatever means had to be employed to accomplish that end.

The violent rejection by the custodians of the ancient revelation of God of Jesus' claim to be the Son of God is one of the
saddest themes in the Gospels. It is developed throughout St.
John's Gospel, in elaboration of his announcement in the Pro-
logue that "He came to his own domain and his own people did
not accept him." Not that all of his own people rejected him!
We have already noted in the early joyful mysteries how the
devout mind formed by the Old Testament in people like Simeon, the shepherds, Joseph and Mary was perfectly adapted to
grasp the meaning of this new and perfect revelation, and to

adore the Word made flesh; but the official custodians of the Old Testament revelation seemed, by contrast, to be of all men the least able to see the glory of God in Jesus Christ. This blindness is portrayed by the evangelists as more than a mere disability: it is culpable wickedness. Our Lord said: "If I had not come, if I had not spoken to them they would have been blameless; but as it is they have no excuse for their sin. Anyone who hates me hates my Father. If I had not performed such works among them as no one else has ever done, they would be blameless; but as it is, they have seen all this, and still they hate both me and my Father" (Jn. 15:22-24).

The Jewish rulers' attack on Jesus was allegedly a defence of the transcendence of God the Father. The evangelists, St. John in particular, declare that any man who really knew the Father and his deeds — and genuine understanding of the Old Testament revelation was the chief means of acquiring such knowledge — would recognize the acts of the Father in the actions of Jesus, and thus be led to accept the mystery of his oneness with the Father. The rulers do not know Jesus because they do not *know* the Father. Their theology is merely theoretical — a matter of words — ; and so, in their ignorance they seek to vindicate the Father's transcendence by convicting the Son of blasphemy.

The scene now shifts to the Roman court. The Gospels give more than a hint that Pontius Pilate, the governor, was impressed with Jesus and wanted to acquit him. First he told the Jews that it was their own domestic affair, and they should try Jesus according to their law. This did not satisfy the Jewish leaders, for they were not allowed to put a man to death — as they reminded Pilate — ; and knowing that Pilate was convinced that Jesus did not deserve to die — "he realised that it was out of jealousy that the chief priests had handed Jesus over" (Mk. 15:10) — they then began to press the charge of sedition. Pilate tried to side-step the issue by offering to release Jesus according to the Passover custom of granting political amnesty to one prisoner. Finally the Jewish leaders put pressure on Pilate by hinting that Rome would be displeased with him if there was an uproar — an uproar which they and not Jesus were set upon fomenting. In effect they told Pilate that it was as much as his job was worth if he did not accede to their request. And so Pilate gave in, knowing that he became accessory to a great crime, but too weak to stand on the truth. His question: "What is truth?" was perhaps a pathetic attempt to plead philosophical scepticism in mitigation of his perfidy.

By a strange irony Pilate's attempt to avoid the issue, by having Jesus scourged in the hope that this might satisfy the chief priests, sets Jesus in immediate association with a dramatic symbol of human weakness and sensuality. The pillar to which Jesus was bound is reminiscent of the sacred pillar of ancient Canaanite worship. The fact that the pillar persists in the traditional imagination of the Church, although it is not mentioned explicitly by the evangelists, may be an indication of its primeval significance for human consciousness. The sacred pillar was an obscene phallic symbol forming part of the apparatus of the cruel and sensual worship that went on at the local shrines in the "high places" in Palestine before the Israelites conquered the land. Indeed, it continued after that time, for it was one of these pillars that Gideon chopped down and burned in defiance of the local gods. This ritual object, like the sacred prostitutes, who were another feature of the Canaanite cults, reminds us of the sensuality and vice that are the motivation of idolatry.

This scene in the Gospel story ends, therefore, not only in terrible physical torture, but in abominable humiliation: the fountain of holiness is bound to an ancient symbol of the most blatant idolatry. Thus humiliated, he takes upon his flesh the punishment for all the sins of human viciousness and sensuality.

Gospel: Mark 15:1-15

The Crowning
with Thorns

Bible-readings

Wisdom 5:1-24	The man we used to laugh at
Jeremiah 14:17-22	"Have you rejected Judah altogether?"
Psalm 88	Wretched, slowly dying
Hebrews 8:1-13	The perfect covenant
Luke 23:8-12	Jesus before Herod
Acts 25:13 - 26:1	The imitation of Christ

Homily

The crowning with thorns is closely connected with the scourging at the pillar. The crowning with thorns and clothing in purple is like the insult that is added to an injury, although, as we saw, the scourging was itself a deep and cruel insult, and the crowning with thorns, although meant primarily as mockery, was also a severe torture. The crowning with thorns, however, is the appropriate climax to a particular idea which runs through the trial before Pilate. In presenting Jesus to Pilate for trial, the Sanhedrin represented the concept of the Christ in political terms — as the national hero who would come to free his people from the Roman yoke. Some among the Jews may have shared in this expectation; others may have been quite happy to leave things as they were and enjoy their privileged position under Roman patronage. Whatever their private views, all agreed, that to portray this man Jesus as one claiming to be the popular Messiah, was the best way to discredit him with the Roman authorities. Pilate could scarcely ignore the charge.

The idea seemed to grip Pilate's imagination. His first question was: "Are you the king of the Jews?"; and, all through the trial, Pilate kept coming back to the concept of kingship, as if, by some mysterious enlightenment, he were beginning to see the deeper meaning of the term, and almost to believe that the description might be accurate. Pilate's strange preoccupation with the phrase "king of the Jews" is shown, too, by his sarcastic comment, "Do you want me to crucify your king?", and by his stubborn refusal to alter the superscription on the cross. When the chief priests complained of the title, "King of the Jews," Pilate answered, "What I have written, I have written."

The crowning with thorns and the clothing in purple is thus a sign of the rejection by both the Jews and the Roman soldiers of the kingship of Christ. To the eye of pride and cruelty, Jesus appeared as an object of contempt: a half-dead human being, dressed up in royal purple, a diadem of sharp thorns on his head, and a reed for scepter in his hand; but to the eye of faith he appeared, and appears, as the "lamb of God that takes away the sin of the world," and the world's true king.

Compared with Matthew, Mark, and John, St. Luke introduces an interesting variation into this part of the Gospel story. We note first that he does not mention the scourging or the crowning directly. This is another example of Luke creating his effect by silence or restraint. Having described the anger of the mob, and told us that in the end Pilate yielded to their demand, he adds the terse and ominous comment that Pilate "handed Jesus over to them to deal with as they pleased."

But we notice also that Luke includes material that is absent from the other three evangelists. St. Luke reports that Pilate, discovering that Jesus was a Galilean, tried to pass responsibility over to Herod Antipas, who was tetrarch of Galilee. In this way a fresh category of people is introduced. Herod was one of the native puppet rulers. He was a Jew, but one who had become Hellenized. That is, he sat loosely to the tradition of his fathers, having succumbed to the allurements of pagan Greek culture. He was a man of the world. We meet him earlier in the Gospel story as the man rebuked by John the Baptist for adultery with his brother's wife, and who then had John the Baptist beheaded. We learn, too, (Mt.14:1-2) that he thought Jesus might be John the Baptist come back from the dead, and he was very anxious to see a miracle. His pleasure now at seeing Jesus for himself was, therefore, completely insincere and worldly. In Herod, our Lord faced the world and Satan and all his empty promises. Herod, indeed, represented the kind of worldliness and sensuality that we saw symbolized in the sacred pillar of Canaanite worship, for he was typical of the Jew who had accommodated himself to the surrounding idolatry. Herod's response to our Lord, in keeping with the frivolity of his life, was contempt and mockery. He had Jesus dressed up in a prince's cloak, ironically and involuntarily acknowledging him as the prince of David's line.

St. Luke tells how on that day Herod and Pilate were reconciled, having previously been enemies. In the Acts of the Apostles — written also by Luke — he refers to this incident, seeing it as the fulfillment of a prophecy in Psalms 2:1-2:

> "Kings on earth setting out to war,
> princes making an alliance,
> against the Lord and against his Anointed (Christ)."
>
> (Acts 4:26)

An even more significant link between St. Luke's Gospel and the book of Acts is the parallel between the record of the passion of our Lord and the story of St. Paul's arrest and trials, recorded at length from chapter 21 of Acts onwards.

The passion story had begun in the Temple, where Jesus taught daily in the days immediately preceding his arrest. His claim to be able to destroy the Temple and rebuild it in three days, and his driving out of those whose job was to change all foreign currency into the Temple coinage were correctly interpreted by the chief priests as an attack upon what the Temple represented, viz., the exclusiveness and finality of the Jewish law and religion. In Acts 21 St. Paul is portrayed in the same role. He is accused of bringing Greeks into the Temple — a violation of Jewish exclusiveness — and in general of preaching everywhere "against the Law and against this place." The accusation is exactly the same as that made against Jesus, that he, in the first place, believes that Jesus is the Son of God, and in his name is declaring the limited scope of the Jewish faith, and pointing to its perfection in the Gospel of the resurrection of Christ. It is because the chief priests and their followers refused to admit this need for fulfillment that they were moved to such fury against both Jesus and Paul.

And so St. Paul suffers the same fate as his Master — even to the detail of the slap on the face. The mob clamor for his death. The Roman police arrest him — for his own safety — and he begins a long period of trial and captivity. The series of trials to which he is subjected before the Sanhedrin, Pilate, and Agrippa, reminds us of the trials of Jesus. The different groups play roughly the same parts: the Sanhedrin persist in demanding the death penalty; the Romans, afraid of the Jews, keep Paul prisoner, although convinced of his innocence; Agrippa takes an academic and supercilious interest in the prisoner.

It is the interlude at Caesarea, where Paul appears before the local ruler King Agrippa, that gives the story a clear affinity with Luke's Gospel. Agrippa was grand-nephew of Herod Antipas of the Gospel story. Like his great-uncle, Agrippa represents the "sophisticated" world, the people who often find religion "interesting," but are ruled, not by its precepts, but by their own inclinations. Footnote "e" to chapter 25 of Acts in the *Jerusalem Bible,* gives a hint of the kind of people Agrippa and his sister Bernice were.

The story of St. Paul's arrest and imprisonment reveals the truth of our Lord's saying: "The disciple is not above his master." It is, in miniature, the story of the Church and of every Christian. Paul had already set foot on the way of the cross, had begun to suffer in the same way and for exactly the same reasons as his Master; but his road to Calvary, like the road taken by most Christians, was to stretch out over many years, in the course of which he was to be given many opportunities of preaching the Gospel. We notice, too, that at his several trials St. Paul's audience were always divided. The chief priests condemned him, some of the Pharisees showed sympathy; Felix, the Roman governor, was divided in his own mind — he listened attentively, but closed his ears to the message when it began to touch him on the raw; Herod Agrippa, in his tentative way, said: "A little more, and your arguments would make a Christian of me." In the end it is not Jesus or Paul or any of the Lord's disciples who are on trial, but those to whom the message is declared. The abject human being in the dock, crowned with thorns and decked out in the mock vestments of royalty, is in reality a member of the new royal and priestly kingdom, enjoying the supreme dignity of those who suffer for the truth's sake.

Gospel: Mark 15:16-20

The Carrying of the Cross

Homily

Once Pilate had handed Jesus over to the chief priests and rulers of the people to do with him what they pleased, the drama was really ended. In the garden, some twelve hours earlier, Jesus had made his perfect self-oblation through the eternal Spirit to his heavenly Father, had offered complete obedience of will, even to death. Man's disobedience and rejection of the Son of God had been finally declared in the trial scenes, the scourging and the mockery. Jesus was as good as dead now. All that remained was to set the external seal upon the living sacrifice of our Lord Jesus Christ.

The evangelists, therefore, do not give a great deal of space to an account of the way of the cross and the crucifixion. They have prepared their readers so well by the preceding scenes and discourses, that there is no need for them to do so. The way of the cross in particular — although it has become the subject of a quite lengthy popular devotion — is described by Matthew in one verse, by Mark in two, and by John in half of a verse. We must realize, however, that the devotion we know as the Stations of the Cross includes the whole meaning of the Passion, and so extends its scope to all of the material we are meditating upon in all of the five sorrowful mysteries of the Rosary. For the moment we will confine our thoughts to what we find in those few verses of the four evangelists in which they describe the road from Pilate's Pavement to Golgotha.

Even in its reticence, the few words about the way of the cross fill in the picture of our Lord's genuine humanity and the reality of his suffering. He has suffered an agony of anticipation and of spiritual torment in the garden; he has suffered excruciating physical pain by a scourging severe enough to kill a weaker man; he has been humiliated and derided; and now he is expected to make a last killing effort to walk up the hill to his death. He is like an athlete being spurred on to run and win a gruelling race when all his strength is already spent. But whereas an athlete would have been rested and had his limbs anointed and massaged in preparation, Jesus had been anointed with blows and massaged on every inch of his body with the sharp teeth of a loaded lash. And whereas an athlete could have looked hopefully beyond the race to rest and refreshment, Jesus could look forward only to being nailed down upon a cross. Having been punished by others, Jesus is now expected to punish himself by putting out the almost impossible effort that will get him up the hill to Calvary.

This brief episode declares the fact that our Lord's divinity never for a moment relieved him of any of the burden which as man he had to carry. It is to impress upon us that Jesus, in his human nature, and without any mitigation from his divine nature, bore all the weight of his cross and what it signified, that St. John says, "carrying his own cross he went out of the city to the place of the skull." The heavenly Father did not spare his only Son — not even when he was at the last gasp. And this implies no callousness on the Father's part, for he, too, was giving — giving his only Son for the sake of the world. The world could not be redeemed without this complete and unassisted sacrifice, and the Father was willing to see it carried out. "God loved the world so much that he gave his only Son . . ." (Jn.3:16). St. John no doubt saw the completeness of our Lord's acceptance of the cross prefigured in the story of the sacrifice of Isaac. There, in Genesis chapter 22, we read that "Abraham took the wood for the burnt offering, loaded it on Isaac, and carried in his own hands the fire and the knife." The son Isaac had to bear the whole brunt of the oblation; and so had Christ.

When we see that it is this theological statement that St. John is making — that the Son, in his human nature, unassisted by the privilege of his oneness with the Father, is carrying the whole weight of the cross — then we will not be bewildered by the report of the other evangelists, all of whom tell us that Simon of Cyrene was enlisted — fairly quickly it seems — to carry the cross for Jesus. St. John, in harmony with the whole method of his Gospel, is making a theological point; the other three evangelists are reporting external facts. Simon of Cyrene carried the cross, but did not thereby in the least alleviate our Lord's sufferings. If he can be said to have assisted our Lord, he assisted him to fill up the cup of his agony by deferring his collapse and death until after he had suffered the final torture of the nails and cramps of crucifixion. Our Lord's executioners were being kind to be cruel. And if Simon did not lessen our Lord's physical suffering, still less can he be said to have assisted in carrying the cross in the sense in which St. John uses that phrase. Nothing that any man can do can lift the least bit of weight of the sin of the world. Only Jesus Christ, Son of God and son of man, can do that. Thus Jesus carried his own cross and carried it alone.

The evangelist who devotes most space to the carrying of the cross is St. Luke. His account runs to seven verses, and includes the report that women of Jerusalem showed compassion on our Lord as he passed by. This little touch is a reminder that although rejection of Jesus in some measure burdens every human conscience, rejection is not the final response to Jesus' revelation of the love of God. These women are a sign of the stirrings of faith, love, and hope. Jesus, for his part, shows compassion on them, and urges them to pray for themselves, for there are dark days ahead. First he alludes to a prophecy of

Hosea telling of how God will punish Israel for its idolatry, then to a prophecy of Ezekiel similarly telling of God's wrath upon Israel, and of how God will send a fire so terrible that it will devour growing green vegetation. How much worse, then, will it be for the dry brushwood that deserves to be burned up?

In this way, in the very moment of his death, our Lord declares his trust in the perfect justice of his Father in heaven. The judgment he is suffering will recoil upon the heads of his accusers, and upon all who remain impenitent and refuse to receive him as Lord. And yet, he does not invoke these warning prophecies as any kind of vengeful threat, but in a tone of solicitous appeal and of hope — as in the final stanza of Psalm 69:

"For God will save Zion,
and rebuild the towns of Judah:
they will be lived in, owned,
handed down to his servants' descendants,
and lived in by those who love his name."

Gospel: Mark 15:21-22

The Crucifixion

Homily

Having reached Golgotha, the place of a skull, Jesus' executioners brutally nailed him down through wrists and ankles to the cross, and then, pushing the cross erect and jolting it into position, left him to die slowly upon it; for our Lord's vicarious sufferings — great as they already had been — would not be complete until he had made the last supreme oblation of life itself.

1. *The atonement*

Jesus had said to his disciples: "A man can have no greater love than to lay down his life for his friends" (Jn. 15:13). Applied to his own self-sacrifice, however, these words of Jesus have a much deeper meaning than appears on the surface, and the comment of one of the criminals crucified beside him gives the clue to that deeper meaning. The "good thief" said to his companion: "We got the same sentence as he did, but in our case we deserved it: we are paying for what we did. But this man

59

has done nothing wrong." The most important thing for us to meditate upon is not that Jesus died an untimely death, but simply that he died, for death is specifically the primeval curse upon sin, and Jesus was completely sinless; and, as if that were not enough, the utter injustice of the condemnation is heightened by the form of his death, for the Jewish Law said: "Cursed be everyone who is hanged upon a tree." Thus behind the outward event of Jesus' death lies a mysterious happening: the payment of a debt by one who in no sense at all incurred that debt. This complete innocence of Jesus, however, allied to the divinity of his person, is what endows that payment with its perfect efficacy to cancel all sin and reconcile mankind with God.

All of the evangelists tell the story of the Crucifixion so as to point clearly to this fact of atonement, of reconciliation between God and man through the sacrifice of Christ in man's place. The inclusion of the two criminals in the crucifixion group is the evangelists' way of recalling the fourth song of the servant of Yahweh (Is. 52:13-53:12) where the prophet speaks of this suffering servant "letting himself be taken for a sinner." It is that song, too, that says:

> "And yet ours were the sufferings he bore,
> ours the sorrows he carried . . .
> Yet he was pierced through for our faults,
> crushed for our sins.
> On him lies the punishment that brings us peace,
> and through his wounds we are healed."

The incongruous trio upon Calvary may also — in the inspired imagination of the evangelists — call to mind the mercy-seat of God within the Holy of Holies — the "propitiatory" — upon which, once a year, the high priest sprinkled the blood of a goat in atonement for the sins of Israel. This mercy-seat — symbol of God's presence — was flanked on each side by the figure of a cherub with wings upraised. In keeping with the inversion of values, which we have seen to characterise all of our Lord's passion, these angelic beings have been changed into two criminals, one on each side of the real presence of God upon the cross — a transformation which symbolizes the derision to which the Son of God was being subjected, as it also symbolizes, ironically, the real depths of God's mercy in stooping so close to sinful men.

The Temple itself, wherein so many propitiatory sacrifices took place, is explicitly mentioned early on in the Crucifixion scene by those who jeered: "So you would destroy the Temple and rebuild it in three days! Then save yourself: come down from the cross!" This unwitting testimony to what is about to happen in a more profound sense in the Resurrection, reminds us that Jesus is the true Temple wherein alone real atonement is taking place.

The seamless robe of Christ, pointedly drawn to our attention when we see the soldiers casting lots for possession of it, is likewise a link with the sacrificial-atonement thought of Jewish religion. The high priest, whose duty it was once a year to enter the Holy of Holies and offer the propitiatory sacrifice, wore just such a robe as this.

The rending of the Temple veil, which occurred at the moment of our Lord's death, is even more significant, for it proclaims that Jesus is at that moment entering once and for all into the real Holy of Holies and making a real, not a symbolic, sacrifice of atonement. This thought is expounded at length in the letter to the Hebrews chapters 7-9.

The atoning power of our Lord's death upon the cross is declared, above all perhaps, by the clear association of the Crucifixion with the feast of the Passover. All of the events of the Passion occurred at Passover time. St. John, in particular, goes out of his way to synchronize exactly the time of the Crucifixion with the time when, in the Temple close by, the priests were slaughtering the paschal lambs for yet another Passover festival. The blood of the paschal lamb, sprinkled on the lintel and doorposts of every Israelite house in Egypt at the first Passover, had caused the Lord to pass over these houses and spare the occupants: so now, the blood of Jesus, shed upon the crossbeam and upright post of the cross, enabled the Lord God at last to pass over all the sins of the new Israel, of those, that is, who believe in the Son of God, hanging upon the cross.

Not only the evangelists, but the New Testament writers generally look back to the death of Jesus as the pivot of redemption, the unique atoning event, without which the forgiving power of God's love could not have achieved its effect upon mankind. St. Peter very simply says: "Christ suffered for you . . . He had not done anything wrong, . . . He was bearing our faults in his own body on the cross, so that we might die to our faults and live for holiness; through his wounds you have been healed" (1 Pet. 2:21-24). The writer to the Hebrews says: "His death took place to cancel the sins that infringed the earlier covenant" (Heb. 9:15). St. Paul says: "He has overridden the Law, and cancelled every record of the debt we had to pay; he has done away with it by nailing it to the cross . . ." (Col. 2:14) and "For our sake God made the sinless one into sin, so that in him we might become the goodness of God" (2 Cor. 5:21).

2. *The manner of our Lord's death*

During the crucifixion — so three of the evangelists tell us — there was an eclipse of the sun. Matthew adds that as Jesus died the earth quaked and the tombs opened to give up the bodies of many holy men. These phenomena had been foretold by the prophets as signs of the day of the Lord. These signs impressed even the Roman soldiers, who declared: "In truth this was a son of God." The mention of the release of men already dead is a symbolic declaration that Christ's atoning death was retrospectively effective for all of the faithful since the world began. St. Peter corroborates this thought by saying: ". . . in the spirit he went to preach to the spirits in prison" (1 Pet. 3:19. cf. also 1 Pet. 4:5,6).

As he hung upon the cross Jesus uttered the opening lines of Psalm 22:

"My God, my God, why have you deserted me?"
The mention of the vinegar, which someone offered him, draws our attention to Psalm 69 also. Both of these Psalms indicate how real was our Lord's human dread and desolation at the prospect of death. In Psalm 69:15 we read:

"Do not let the waves wash over me,
  do not let the deep swallow me
    or the Pit close its mouth on me."

Once again we have proof of how our Lord drained the cup of human suffering to the dregs, with no mitigation by reason of his divinity. Perhaps we may see our Lord's final sip of vinegar, as recorded by St. John, as his symbolic draining of this cup of bitterness to the dregs.

If, however, we read these two Psalms right through, we discover that both end in a note of triumph. Psalm 22 ends thus:

"The whole earth, from end to end, will remember and
    come back to Yahweh;
all the families of the nations will bow down before him.
For Yahweh reigns, the ruler of nations!
Before him all the prosperous of the earth will bow down,
before him will bow all who go down to the dust.
And my soul will live for him, my children will serve him;
men will proclaim the Lord to generations still to come,
his righteousness to a people yet unborn. All this he has
    done."

All of the evangelists declare this triumph by the manner in which they describe the actual moment of our Lord's death. Matthew, Mark, and Luke say that Jesus cried out in a loud voice and gave up his spirit. Luke tells us that he said: "Father, into your hands I commend my spirit" — one of the night prayers for Jewish children, that his mother would have once taught him. St. John reports that he said: "It is accomplished," and adds that, "bowing his head he gave up his spirit." All of these descriptions convey the impression that there was something deliberate and positive about our Lord's dying. It was an act he performed, not a calamity he suffered. St. John's phrase "bowing his head" is significant, for, it is said, once the head of a victim on a cross fell forward, breathing would cease almost immediately. His sufferings complete, and with the prospect now of merely struggling to enjoy a few minutes more of semiconscious life, Jesus submitted actively and willingly to death by bowing his head in trust and adoration before his Father in heaven, rather than letting it fall as it were against his will. This description and the interpretation of it are perfectly in harmony with our Lord's saying recorded in John 10:17-18.

> "The Father loves me,
> because I lay down my life
> in order to take it up again.
> No one takes it from me;
> I lay it down of my own free will, . . ."

Another important detail is the picture of Jesus breathing out his last breath. In this we have a hint of the new life of the Spirit emanating from him in his death and resurrection, and passing on into his new people. This allusion to the new life of the Church is expressed more explicitly in two ways by St. John. First he depicts Mary, the mother of Jesus, at the foot of the cross in company with the beloved disciple — who may well have been the evangelist himself. In our study of the infancy story we learned that Mary was the perfect flowering of the Old Testament. She had learned all that the Lord had been teaching his ancient people of Israel. Through this perfection she had been counted worthy to bear the Son of God, the Savior of the world. Now, as that Son is dying and in the act of opening the gates of new life to his new Israel, he declares that his own mother must also be the mother of that new people, typified by John, the beloved disciple. As he had been dependent upon her initial consent before he could take flesh and so become equipped with the means of redeeming mankind, so the Church, his many brethren, were equally dependent upon that same consent of hers, continuing its efficacy in respect of the members of Christ's body through her perpetual intercession.

The other mention of the Church to come is in the episode of the piercing of our Lord's side, when blood and water flowed out. This is a dramatic illustration of the fact that the Church, dependent for its life upon the sacraments of baptism and the eucharist, is truly one in being with the very flesh and blood of

Christ. There is a real flesh and blood connexion, not just a moral connexion, between Christ and his mystical body.

We began our meditation upon our Lord's coming to earth, by using the text of St. Luke's Gospel. In meditating now upon our Lord's last few hours upon earth it is fitting that we should turn in conclusion to that same Gospel. St. Luke continues the note of hope that we observed in his account of the way of the cross. One of the thieves appears contrite and is promised entry into paradise. The centurion ends up saying: "This was a great and good man," and the crowd go home "beating their breats." Joseph of Arimathea appears — representing those among the Jewish leaders who had not consented to the condemnation of Jesus, and who were potential converts to the new Israel — and gives Jesus a temporary but very costly burial (cf. Jn. 19:39) in a tomb close by the place of execution ("They gave him a grave with the wicked, a tomb with the rich" — Is. 53:9). With a keen instinct for artistic unity, St. Luke, having at the beginning of his narrative pictured Mary and Joseph wrapping the babe in swaddling clothes and laying him in a manger, rounds the story off with a picture of Joseph, another just man, wrapping Jesus in the bands of a linen shroud and laying him in a tomb. But Luke's sense of unity is theological as well as artistic. The story ends with the sentence: "And on the sabbath day they rested, as the Law required." Not only did God's servants rest, but God himself — as after the six days of creation — now rested, for his work of re-creation was complete.

Gospel: Mark 15:23-47

Part Three

THE GLORIOUS
MYSTERIES

The Resurrection

Homily

All through his Gospel, St. John looks forward to our Lord's being raised up on the cross as his true glorification. Jesus had said: "The Son of Man must be lifted up . . . so that everyone who believes may have eternal life in him" (Jn. 3:13-15); "When you have lifted up the Son of Man, then you will know that I am He" (Jn. 8:28); "And when I am lifted up from the earth, I shall draw all men to myself" (Jn. 12:32). And on the eve of his death Jesus began his great priestly prayer with these words: "Father, the hour has come (i.e. of his own death): glorify your Son so that your Son may glorify you" (Jn. 17:1). These sayings point to the Crucifixion as the triumphant climax of our Lord's work, the point where the Father would be supremely glorified in the Son. Consistent with this thought is John's emphasis upon our Lord's final cry from the cross: "It is accomplished."

The power of the Resurrection was thus latent in the triumph of the cross; but the disciples did not yet understand what was going on, even although our Lord had forewarned them of what would happen to him. For them Jesus was simply dead and buried; the victory of the cross still had to be revealed to them. The record of that revelation, and comment on what precisely such a revelation involved, are contained in the concluding chapters of the four Gospels.

The sabbath rest over, some of the women went to the tomb with spices, expecting to find the corpse of Jesus. To their amazement they found the stone rolled away and the tomb empty. Thereupon two angels appeared to them and told them that Jesus had risen from the dead. The women returned and told the apostles what they had seen and heard, but the apostles regarded their story as "pure nonsense" (Lk. 24:11). St. Luke reports that "Peter, however, went running to the tomb. He bent down and saw the binding clothes but nothing else; he then went back home, amazed at what had happened." This amazement does not seem to have amounted to understanding or belief. Later in the same day the Lord appeared to two disciples on the road to Emmaus, but these two did not recognize him. He said to them: "You foolish men! So slow to believe the full message of the prophets!" On the evening of the same day, when Jesus appeared to the assembled company of apostles, these, too, did not immediately believe it was he, but thought that they were seeing a ghost.

These records in the Gospels teach us that to believe in the risen Lord is not a matter simply of physical sight. Seeing is not necessarily believing. The parable of the rich man and the begger (Lk. 16) is about this very problem. The rich man asks for the beggar to be sent back from the dead to warn his brothers to mend their ways. He is told: "They have Moses and the prophets, let them listen to them . . . If they will not listen to Moses or to the prophets, they will not be convinced even if someone should rise from the dead." That is why our Lord had to elicit the faith of the two disciples on the road to Emmaus, and of the company of apostles, by expounding for them the meaning of the scriptures (Lk. 24:25-27; 44-46) for no miracle, not even his own rising from the dead can convince any man unless, through his diligent attention to the word of God as it has been declared to mankind since time began, and through prayer, he has ac-

quired the disposition that is able to blossom into full faith in
Jesus as Lord.

For us who live two thousand years after the Resurrection
this is a comforting fact. It means that we are no less, and no
more, capable of finding true faith in our risen Lord than were
those who saw him with their own eyes. The power to believe
comes from an inner understanding of the meaning of our
Lord's death and Resurrection. This understanding, this faith, is
something we must pray for, because, as our Lord said: "No
one can come to me unless he is drawn by the Father who sent
me" (Jn. 6:44).

St. John tells us that Peter was accompanied to the tomb by
"the other disciple, the one Jesus loved," and that this disciple
— almost certainly John himself — going in after Peter, "saw
and believed." This, then, is the record of the first act of true
belief in the risen Lord — and it took place, significantly, on the
evidence of the empty tomb, not on the evidence of sight of the
risen Lord. What was it that John believed? Not simply that
Jesus had been resuscitated, as Lazarus had been, so that he
could enjoy a few more years in the company of his friends, but
that he was truly what he had claimed to be: the Son of God,
now risen to enjoy eternal life.

St. John's report of our Lord's appearance to Mary Magdalene very early in the morning — just after his own act of
belief — brings out the same point. At first she did not recognize him, but after he had addressed her by name she responded
with the cry, "Rabbuni!" This form of address was reserved for
God alone, and so it is her profession of faith in the risen Jesus
as the Son of God.

St. John concludes the main part of his Gospel with a report of our Lord's appearance after a week to St. Thomas who
had previously doubted the testimony of the other apostles.
Thomas' final response is the same: "My Lord and my God."
Faith is fundamentally belief that Jesus is truly God's own Son,
crucified and now returned to enjoy his eternal glory with the
Father, joined with complete subjection of mind, heart, and will
to him as Lord. Jesus' reply to Thomas' declaration of faith underlines what we noted already, that faith can come equally to

men of all times in response to the testimony of the apostles, and is not dependent upon natural sight. St. John thus concludes his story by saying that it was to invite others in all ages to share this life-giving faith that he has recorded a selection of the "signs that Jesus worked." "These are recorded so that you may believe that Jesus is the Christ, the Son of God, and that believing this you may have life through his name" (Jn. 20:31).

In these concluding words St. John declares the purpose behind all the mysterious events that have culminated in the glory of Christ's Resurrection: that believers may share in this new life of the risen Lord. It is no accident, therefore, that our Lord appeared to Mary Magdalene in a garden, and sent her with a message to "the brothers" — the only time, according to St. John, that Jesus used that word of his disciples. Our Lord's victory over death was not a private reward but a victory to be shared with all his brothers; and that gift consisted in taking them back to the state of innocence which man had enjoyed in the garden of Eden. Thus our Lord's atoning sacrifice is seen, especially from the perspective of the Resurrection, as no legal fiction, but as a real reinstatement of mankind in his primeval state. This is the foundation of the new life in the Spirit, of which St. Paul has so much to say in his letters, and about which we must continue to meditate as we turn our thoughts to Christ's return to heavenly glory.

Gospel: John 20:1-31

The Ascension

Bible-readings

Hebrews 1:1-4	Gone to take his place
1 Timothy 3:16	The faith in a nutshell
John 5:19-30	The Judgement
Philippians 2:6-11	Jesus is Lord
Ephesians 5:1-20	Follow Christ by loving
Colossians 3:1-17	A heavenly mind

Homily

The temptation to "freeze" separate scenes in the story of man's redemption is perhaps nowhere more sedulously to be resisted than in respect of the mysteries of the Rosary entitled Crucifixion, Resurrection, and Ascension. All three together make up the revelation of God's glory in his Son, Jesus Christ, and of the mystery of eternal life shed into the hearts of men. With the cross we associate principally the atonement, the making up for the sins of all mankind. St. Paul writes: "God dealt with sin by sending his own Son in a body as physical as any sinful body, and in that body condemned sin. He did this in order that the Law's just demands might be satisfied in us . . ." (Rm. 8:3-4). With the Resurrection we associate principally the victory of Christ's sacrificial death, his own restoration to life, and the prospect of our sharing in that sinless life such as man originally was intended to possess. "If the Spirit of him who raised Jesus from the dead is living in you, then he who raised Jesus from the

dead will give life to your own mortal bodies through his Spirit living in you" (Rm. 8:11). With the Ascension we associate principally our looking ahead to the time when heaven and earth pass away and Christ comes again to judge mankind, and when we, the process of our sanctification complete, will come to share in Christ's glory in heaven. "Blessed be the God and Father of our Lord Jesus Christ, who in his great mercy has given us a new birth as his sons, by raising Jesus Christ from the dead, so that we have a sure hope and the promise of an inheritance that can never be spoilt or soiled and never fade away, because it is being kept for you in the heavens" (1 Pet. 1:3-4).

The Ascension, the final farewell of the Lord to the world of time and space, was the logical conclusion to his glorification through death and resurrection. His presence with the disciples in their visible and tangible world was clearly a temporary episode, sufficient to complete the revelation to men of the mystery of the Word made flesh. The evangelists do not, therefore, spend much time describing this episode. St. Matthew merely records our Lord's final commission to the apostles: "Go, therefore, make disciples of all nations; baptize them in the name of the Father and of the Son and of the Holy Spirit, and teach them to observe all the commands I gave you. And know that I am with you always; yes, to the end of time" (Mt. 28:19-20), and does not mention any departure incident. Mark ends his story similarly, but adds that the Lord "was taken up into heaven" after he had commissioned the apostles. Luke records the command to wait in Jerusalem until they had received power from on high, and then briefly describes how he blessed them and "was carried up to heaven." St. John is silent about the Ascension: he has already told us sufficient to make the Ascension an inevitable conclusion we can draw for ourselves. In the Acts of the Apostles St. Luke repeats his account of the Ascension, ending with the comment of two angels: "Why are you men from Galilee standing here looking up into the sky? Jesus who has been taken up from you into heaven, this same Jesus will come back in the same way as you have seen him go there" — as much as to say: "He is gone for good; it is up to you to get on with the job of preaching his gospel throughout the world, and getting yourselves ready for the day of judgment, when you will see him again."

Meditation on the Ascension ends up, therefore, not in dreamy star-gazing, but in practical consideration of how the life of the Spirit really works out in our lives here on earth. And that is quite simply because the life of the Spirit — the life of heaven, that is — is not something that will begin in the hereafter, but something that begins the moment we are baptized, and goes on until it merges into the timeless life of heaven. St. John reports our Lord's saying: "Whoever listens to my words and believes in the one who sent me, has eternal life . . . the hour will come — in fact it is here already — when the dead will hear the voice of the Son of God, and all who hear it will live" (Jn. 5:24-25). St. Paul, too, links Christ's Resurrection with the life we live while still on this earth. "If the Spirit of him who raised Jesus from the dead is living in you, then he who raised Jesus from the dead will give life to your own mortal bodies through his Spirit living in you" (Rm. 8:11).

St. Paul, whose letters make up roughly one quarter of the New Testment, is writing nearly all the time about the reality of the life we now live by the power of the Holy Spirit, a life that begins in the innocence conferred through faith and baptism and proceeds, through many struggles and setbacks, towards only one goal: perfection — the perfection that we hope to be able to present before our Lord when he comes to be our judge. But St. Paul's teaching is anything but a type of dreary moralism. The point from which he starts is that moralism — striving to keep the Law by our own unaided efforts — has miserably failed and always will fail, because man in his natural state is powerless to please God by keeping the Law, so that the Law in the end can only condemn him, although the Law itself is "sacred, and what it commands is sacred, just and good" (Rm. 7:12). At the heart of St. Paul's insistent and repeated exhortations to seek perfection: "Be like children of the light, for the effects of the light are seen in complete goodness and right living and truth" (Eph. 5:8-9) is the declaration that the new life from which such perfect goodness flows comes as a free gift from God, appropriated only through faith and baptism — "It is by

faith and through Jesus that we have entered this state of grace"
(Rm. 5:2). Faith and baptism provide the mystical but real link
between the believer and the purifying power of Christ's sacrifice — that "union with Christ" by which we "have imitated his
death" (Rm. 6:5) — and into the soul thus purified God is able
to pour the life of the Spirit, so that the Christian can say: "I
have been crucified with Christ, and I live now not with my own
life but with the life of Christ who lives in me" (Gal. 2:19-20).

St. Paul thus resolves any tension there might seem to be
between faith and good works. He stresses, on the one hand,
that atonement is the work of Christ alone, and that we benefit
from that atonement purely by God's free gift, grasped through
faith. On the other hand he insists that this justification by faith
is a real re-creation of our beings, which must issue in a life of
moral perfection, a life, however, that must always be acknowl-
edged as the life of Christ in us. "When we were baptized we
went into the tomb with him and joined him in death, so that as
Christ was raised from the dead by the Father's glory, we to
might live a new life" (Rm. 6:4). Our mystical union with Christ,
crucified, risen, and ascended, is the foundation of St. Paul's
message — of the gospel. Primarily this is a message of life: "Let
your thoughts be on heavenly things, not on the things that are
on the earth, because you have died, and now the life you have is
hidden with Christ in God. But when Christ is revealed — and
he is our life — you too will be revealed in all your glory with
him" (Col. 3:2-4).

Gospel: Luke 24:44-53

The Descent
of the Holy Spirit

Bible-readings

Exodus 24:12-18	The old covenant
Jeremiah 31:31-34	A law written in their hearts
Romans 5:1-11	The Spirit of love
1 Corinthians 12:4-30	The Spirit of unity
1 John 4:19 - 5:4	Love of God and love of neighbour
Acts 2:1-36	The new covenant

Homily

In the first three mysteries of the Rosary the ancient people of God figure prominently in the scheme of salvation. This people and their history were God's word to mankind, and the preparation for the Incarnation of God's Son, the Word made flesh. In the last three mysteries of the Rosary, once again our minds are turned back to the people of God, but this time to the people of the new covenant, those in whom the Lord dwells for ever by his Holy Spirit, thus realizing in the fullest way possible the meaning of the ancient name of the Redeemer: Immanuel, God with us. Because Jesus has returned to his proper place at the right hand of the Father, it is important for us to understand that the perpetual presence which Christ promised his faithful is his presence in them through the Holy Spirit. The life of the people of the old covenant had centered round the presence of God in the Shekinah above the ark of the covenant: the life of the people of the new covenant is nourished by the real sacramental

79

presence of Christ in the eucharist, and manifested in the people themselves, who are Christ's permanent presence on earth, as in a living temple. One of the neatest expressions of this fact is given by St. Peter, who exhorts us in these words: "Set yourselves close to him so that you too, the holy priesthood that offers the spiritual sacrifices which Jesus Christ has made acceptable to God, may be living stones making a spiritual house" (1 Pet.2:5).

It is, of course, the indwelling of the Holy Spirit, which makes the mystical union between the believer and Christ and his redemptive acts a reality. For this reason we should find it helpful to supplement our thoughts about the coming of the Holy Spirit — which we usually derive chiefly from the record in the Acts of the Apostles — with a consideration of this mystery as presented in the Gospels. We have already noted how, in dying, Jesus cried out with a loud voice "and gave up his spirit," and that this indicates the passing on of his Spirit to his disciples. We should note also that St. John includes what amounts to a Pentecost scene among the Resurrection appearances of Jesus on the very first Easter evening. Having greeted the apostles, he said: "As the Father sent me, so I am sending you." Then he breathed on them and continued: "Receive the Holy Spirit. For those whose sins you forgive, they are forgiven; for those whose sins you retain, they are retained." Connected with these accounts we should recall also the episode of the piercing of our Lord on the cross, when blood and water flowed from his side. All of these incidents emphasize the fact that the life of the Church flows from Christ crucified and risen, that the Holy Spirit is *his* Spirit, that the Church is flesh of his flesh and bone of his bone — truly his mystical body. Mystical union with Christ and his redemptive acts means membership in his mystical body, which is the body of flesh and blood enlivened by the Holy Spirit of Christ. The new life of the Spirit really begins in the individual at the moment of his baptism, and the new being thus engendered increases in substance by feeding on the substance of Jesus Christ, true God and true man, under the sacramental signs of his body and blood in the eucharist.

If the message of the birth of the Church through the gift of the Holy Spirit is told in essence in the context of the Resurrection; if, indeed, the Church might be said to have issued from the side of Christ upon the cross — just as Genesis tells us that Eve was made from Adam's rib while he slept — why the additional dramatic story of the birth of the Church at Pentecost, seven weeks after the Resurrection?

On the day of Pentecost the full significance of the indwelling of the Holy Spirit was impressed upon the apostles, and the power of the Spirit in the life of the Church manifested to the world. The very fact that this public manifestation took place at Pentecost — the Jewish feast of Weeks — is of prime importance. Just as the death of Jesus had been linked with the Passover, so the birth of the Church has been linked with the feast which both celebrated the wheat harvest, and commemorated the giving of the Law to Moses on Sinai. There is an interesting parallelism between the New Testament account of Pentecost and the account of Moses on mount Sinai. Before going up the mountain, Moses said to the elders of the people: "Wait here for us until we come back to you" (Ex.24:14); then he went up to meet God on Sinai, returning forty days later bringing the tablets of the Law with him. So in the New Testament, before ascending to his Father, Jesus said to the apostles: "Stay in the city then, until you are clothed with the power from on high" (Lk. 24:49); then on the day of Pentecost, the festival of the Law, he returned to his people in the power of the Holy Spirit. Thus the details, and St. Luke's manner, of telling the story teach us that the birth of the Church is the ratifying of the new covenant with the new people of God, and their being commissioned to set out upon their pilgrimage of bearing witness to the love of God.

Throughout the New Testament the Holy Spirit is constantly spoken of as the Spirit of love, and love is the chief mark of the disciples of Christ. The New Testament emphasis on love develops out of the idea of the new covenant made at Pentecost with the new Israel. The prophet Jeremiah had proclaimed: "The days are coming — it is Yahweh who speaks — when I will make a new covenant with the House of Israel. . . . Deep within them I will plant my Law." The Law of God will, under the new covenant, no longer be regarded as an external constraint, but as the mind and heart of God in which his people share, because they possess his Spirit. Love of God's commandments flows from this real communion with God made possible by Christ's gift of his Spirit; and love of one's neighbor — so certain a sign of love of God — is itself an immediate product of the unseen love of God, which consists in perfect and joyful obedience to his commandments: "We can be sure that we love God's children if we love God himself and do what he has commanded us" (1 Jn.5:2).

The other great sign of the Spirit is unity. This thought, so much in evidence in St. Paul's letters, is present also in the picture of the Church presented by Acts, for there we see the Church manifest as a coherent body, full of mutual respect, its structure firmly held together by the special competences conferred by the Spirit upon different functionaries. St. Paul lists a number of these different offices in 1 Cor. 12:27-28, naming as the three most important: apostles, prophets, teachers. These various gifts are permanent features of the visible Church, all truly spiritual in origin, all necessary for the perfecting of God's purposes. And all these gifts are manifestations not of human qualities or authority, but of love which has its origin in Christ himself, from whom the Spirit flows. "If we live by the truth and in love, we shall grow in all ways into Christ who is the head by whom the whole body is fitted and joined together, every joint adding its own strength, for each separate part to work according to its function. So the body grows until it has built itself up, in love" (Eph.4:15-16).

Gospel: John 14:1-21

The Assumption

Bible-readings

Genesis 3:14-16   The first woman
Exodus 19:3-8   On eagle's wings
The Song of Songs 6:4-10   My dove is unique
Hebrews 3:7 - 4:11   How to reach the land of true promise
John 19:25-27   Mother of the Church
Revelation 12:1-6; 13-17   A place of safety

Homily

The third last mystery of the Rosary turned our thoughts back to the people of God generally, to the whole mystical body of Christ; the last two mysteries direct our minds to a single member of the mystical body — to Mary the mother of God. But Mary is not simply a single member of the Church: she is a singular member, and her singularity was notably confirmed by her exemption from the corruption that is the fate of all other mortals, and by her passing, soul and body, into heavenly glory at the end of her life on earth.

We have already, in the Annunciation and the Visitation, meditated upon the unique role our Lady played in the scheme of man's salvation. Her response to the angelic salutation was the expression of a soul that had been preserved from the first moment of life in a state of primeval innocence; for what was required of her was an act that would exactly correspond to, and fully counterbalance, the act of disobedience freely made by

83

Eve, her will still unflawed by sin. Eve's faithlessness — her acceptance of Satan's word in place of God's — prepared the way for the sin of all mankind: Mary's faithfulness — her recognition that the angel's message was from God, and her believing the promise made to her — prepared the way for the redemption of all mankind, through the self-oblation of the second Adam, the Word made flesh in her womb.

There is a brief episode recorded by Matthew, Mark, and Luke, which tells how our Lord reacted when told that his mother and kinsmen were waiting to see him. St. Luke significantly links the episode with the parable of the Sower, which describes the different types of response men make to the word of God. Our Lord's immediate reaction was to say: "my mother and my brothers are those who hear the word of God and put it into practice" (Lk.8:19-21) thus pointing to the essential quality that made Mary his mother; hearing and obeying the word of God. Similarly, discipleship consists in learning to practice this discernment and obedience which Mary had practised perfectly all her life.

Mary's act of obedience is thus a vital factor in the scheme of man's redemption, so vital that she can be said to have co-operated with God in the work of redemption. Thus, towards the end of the second century, Irenaeus Bishop of Lyons could write: "The knot of Eve's disobedience was untied by Mary's obedience. What the virgin Eve bound through her unbelief, Mary loosed by her faith"; and even more strongly: "Being obedient, she became the cause of salvation for herself and for the whole human race."

We must remember, of course, that Mary, too, was redeemed. As the Second Vatican Council (Constitution on the Church, n. 53) says: "Because she belongs to the offspring of Adam she is one with all human beings in their need for salvation." Her salvation, like that of all men, resulted from God's favor, and was accomplished through the merits of Christ's sacrifice, in her case applied from the moment of her conception; and the primary reason for her preservation from the decaying effects of sin was so that Christ could assume a perfect human nature. In Mary, fully redeemed by his own merits, he prepared a body for himself.

Her perfection of soul and body, however, conferred a unique privilege upon Mary herself. "Because of this gift of sublime grace she far surpasses all other creatures, both in heaven and on earth" (Constitution on the Church, n. 53); and her passing directly from life upon earth to heavenly glory was the logical consequence of her sinlessness — her fullness of grace. Having no stain of sin upon her, Mary had no need to pay the penalty of sin, which is death. She could pass immediately from the finitude of this life to the glorious life of the resurrection. This is what is meant by Mary's Assumption into heaven.

In earlier meditations we traced the Church's doctrine concerning our Lady back to the meaning of scripture, in particular to the Gospel of the infancy presented by St. Luke. We can now complete the picture by turning to one who, after our Lord, was closest to Mary: the beloved disciple, St. John, to whose care Mary was commended by her dying Son. St. John went to live at Ephesus, and there, among the local congregation with whom our Lady lived, John or one of his close friends wrote the book of Revelation which, among its many visions, contains one which may well be John's pictorial expansion, on a cosmic canvas, of that never-to-be-forgotten scene at the foot of the cross — a scene with four characters: Mary the mother, her Saviour-Son, John representing all her other children, and the great enemy of mankind, the primeval serpent.

The vision referred to is contained in Revelation chapter 12, vv 1-6 & 13-17 (the intervening verses seem to be a separate vision). The vision opens with the appearance of a great sign in Heaven: "a woman, adorned with the sun, standing on the moon." She is pregnant and cries aloud in childbirth. Here is an allusion to Eve, who was to bring forth in pain and from whom one would come who would bruise the serpent's head. A dragon now appears and lies in wait to devour the child at birth; but the child is taken up to God and to his throne. The woman, too, escapes into the desert where God has prepared a place for her.

So far the vision is reminiscent of the Old Testament. Israel had given birth to the great leader Moses who escaped from the dragon of the Nile-Pharaoh to be taken safely into the palace of the king, while eventually Israel herself escaped into the wilderness. At the same time, the imagery cannot but be seen as applying to Christ and his Ascension to the Father. The image of the dragon lying in wait can thus be legitimately applied to Satan seeking to destroy Christ, both at the moment of his birth (the slaughter of the innocents) and at the moment of his Crucifixion.

The escape of the child into heaven (Resurrection and Ascension) must have been what caused the dragon to find himself thrown down to the earth, and provoked him now to direct his attack upon the woman. The second paragraph of the vision makes a fresh start and the woman becomes the central figure — although she has already been taken to a place of safety when she seemed to symbolize Israel. This move to a second phase is what justifies us in thinking that now — with the confused logic of dreams — the image of the woman has assumed a second and more individualized meaning. From this assault, however, she is delivered, being borne up on "a huge pair of eagle's wings." Eagle's wings represent the protection of God himself (Ex. 19:4; Dt.32:11). The woman, therefore, can be said to have been completely removed from all possibility of Satan's assault by the intervention of God himself. Although, according to the vision, the woman is completely out of reach, the dragon, in a fit of final fury, vomits a river of water after her, but the river is swallowed up by the earth. This additional piece of action only serves to underline the total invulnerability the woman now enjoys. Enraged at his double failure — both with the child and his mother — Satan now turns to make war on "the rest of her children." The writer spells out for us who these are: "All who obey God's commandments and bear witness for Jesus," that is the whole Church on earth.

The vision, especially in its second phase, would seem, therefore, to give a unique distinction to "the woman" in contrast to "the rest of her children." They live out their lives in the period of persecution that is this world's history: she, invulnerable to Satan's attack, already enjoys complete safety in a place prepared for her by God. Her deliverance is comparable to the ascension of her child, who "was taken straight up to Gcd and to his throne."

Gospel: Luke 8:4-8 & 19-21

Crowning of Our Lady in Heaven

Bible-readings

Judith 13:18-20	The glory of Jerusalem
Psalm 45:10-17	Ancestors replaced by sons
1 John 3:1-9	God's seed in us
2 Peter 1:3-11	Sharing the divine nature
Hebrews 12:18-29	Gathered for the festival
Revelation 7:9-17	Palm in their hands

Homily

The heart and centre of the Rosary is quite plainly the great mystery of our Lord's redemptive action, focussed on the events that took place between the first Holy Thursday and Pentecost. That is why, after the first three mysteries, our Lady falls more or less into the background, for her primary purpose, that of bearing the Redeemer of the world, has been fulfilled. It is appropriate, however, that it is at the beginning and at the end of the meditation that she does enjoy prominence, because she provides the human framework around her Son's redemptive work. In the Annunciation we took note of how, by her perfect discernment of, and obedience to, the word of God she provided the human link in the chain of redemptive events; now we take note of her final reward: her Assumption into heaven, and her crowning as Queen of angels and saints.

In considering this final glory of our Lady we ought first to observe that the honor conferred upon her was indeed *con-*

ferred. Christ, by the power of his own divinity, and by right, *ascended* to resume the glory that was his with the Father before time began: our Lady *was assumed* into heaven and given glory by divine favor, for, as we noted in the last meditation, "she is one with all human beings in their need for salvation." Secondly, we ought to observe that, although our Lady is one of the redeemed, there never was a moment in her life that she was not redeemed. This enabled her to anticipate, as it were, the general resurrection, and enjoy perfect bliss of body and soul from the moment her life on earth was over. But in so doing she realized perfectly the goal towards which the whole Church is moving. "Therefore she is hailed as a pre-eminent and altogether singular member of the Church, and as the Church's model and excellent exemplar in faith and charity" (Constitution on the Church, n. 53).

The New Testament speaks in many places and in many phrases of this "glory, as yet unrevealed, which is waiting for us" (Rm. 8:18). It is no less than the radiance of the image of the Son of God. Of the redeemed St. Paul writes: "They are the ones he chose specially long ago and intended to become true images of his Son, so that his Son might be the eldest of many brothers. He called those he intended for this; those he called he justified, and with those he justified he shared his glory" (Rm. 8:29-30). The New Testament speaks also of the transfiguration of our mortal bodies, so that the bodily Assumption of our Lady can be seen as an earnest of the resurrection of the other members of the mystical body of Christ. "The dead will be raised, imperishable, and we shall be changed as well, because our present perishable nature must put on imperishability and this mortal nature must put on immortality" (1 Cor. 15:52-53).

Therefore, while venerating our Lady's pre-eminence among the redeemed, we need not, and must not, picture her in isolation. She is the supreme glory of the heavenly Jerusalem, but that city is a place where "millions of angels have gathered for the festival, with the whole Church in which everyone is a 'first-born son' and a citizen of heaven" (Heb. 12:22).

The Constitution on the Church (n. 65) points out that "In the most holy Virgin the Church has already reached that perfec-

tion whereby she exists without spot or wrinkle. Yet the followers of Christ still strive to increase in holiness by conquering
sin." In the vision of St. John of the woman adorned with the
sun (Rev. 12:1-6; 13-17) we learned how the woman escaped to a
place of complete safety, whereas the rest of her children —
those other than Christ himself — were left to face the assault of
Satan. This persecution will harass the Church until the end of
time. "Because you do not belong to the world, because my
choice withdrew you from the world, therefore the world hates
you" (Jn. 15:19).

We tend to think of persecution as physical torments such
as the early Christians, whom St. John knew, suffered at the
hands of the Roman empire. This is certainly part of what is
meant, for such torment is a severe trial of faith. But it is more
than that. St. John — like the other New Testament writers —
makes quite clear in his letters, that the struggle with Satan goes
on all the time in the soul of man, even when there is no appar-
ent outward persecution; and the particular historical persecu-
tions to which St. John may allude in his Revelation thus become symbols of the constant interior persecution of the Church
by Satan. "My children, do not let anyone lead you astray: to
live a holy life is to be holy just as he is holy; to lead a sinful life
is to belong to the devil" (1 Jn. 3:7-8). Faith and baptism re-
create our souls, but the struggle between the word of God and
the empty promises of Satan goes on in our members until the
final victory is won; and there can be no relaxation of vigilance
for the individual until his own personal judgment is past, nor
for the Church until the last day.

One of the most sustained exhortations to perseverance in
faith and faithfulness is contained in the letter to the Hebrews,
beginning at chapter eleven with the familiar sentence: "Only
faith can guarantee the blessings that we hope for, or prove the
existence of the realities that at present remain unseen." The
writer takes our thoughts right back to Abraham, father of the
faithful, and sees in the nomadic life he accepted in response to
God's call a symbol of the life of the Church. "For there is no
eternal city for us in this life but we look for one in the life to
come" (13:14). Most important, perhaps, is his reminder of

what is the mainspring of true religion: recognizing and obeying the word of God. "Make sure," he says, "that you never refuse to listen when he speaks" (12:25). This was precisely how Abraham proved himself. Thus he became father of a vast nation, the most illustrious member of which was Mary who in her time displayed the qualities of her ancestor, but in a pre-eminent degree, so that she became the mother of an even vaster nation — of the whole Church of God. Blessed as she had been in her ancestor, she became even more blessed in her offspring, first of whom was no other than the Son of the most high God.

> "Your ancestors will be replaced by sons
> whom you will make lords of the whole world" (Ps. 45:16).

It is on this thought of the universal motherhood of Mary that we shall close. Her willingly accepted motherhood of the Redeemer was, by the pleasure of God, a vital link in the scheme of our salvation — "the cause of salvation" as St. Irenaeus so strongly expresses it. So, too, she continues to perform a maternal office in the life of "the rest of her children" corporately and individually. Her perpetual intercession is a vital link in the process of our sanctification. The Second Vatican Council teaches that Mary's maternity "will last without interruption until the eternal fulfilment of all the elect. For, taken up to heaven, she did not lay aside this saving role, but by her manifold acts of intercession continues to win for us gifts of eternal salvation" (Constitution on the Church, n. 62). The Council reminds us that "The maternal duty of Mary in no way obscures or diminishes this unique mediation of Christ, but rather shows its power. For all the saving influences of the Blessed Virgin on men originate, not from some inner necessity, but from the divine pleasure. They flow forth from the superabundance of the merits of Christ . . ." (n. 60).

We ought never to forget that, according to St. John, the first "sign" our Lord performed, and by which he "let his glory be seen," was performed at his mother's instigation — the changing of water into wine at the wedding-feast at Cana. This "sign" is of the deepest significance. It was a declaration of the whole essence of redemption, a prelude to his whole ministry. "They have no wine": the human race — even the chosen people — have lost the joy of the life of grace. Our Lord points out that his "hour" has not come: that loss cannot be made good until the hour of his passion, death, and glorification is past. None the less he gives a "sign" that this restoration will be accomplished; and at this first "sign," wherein he manifests his glory, he allowed his divine action to follow his mother's intercession. This in itself was a "sign" of his mother's part in the scheme of redemption.

If our Lord did not feel his power and glory diminished by accepting her subsidiary efforts of love, why should we hesitate to invoke that same interceding love in order to obtain, not just this or that trivial favor, but the wine of supernatural life in full measure — the perfect sanctification of our souls, the redemption of the whole world?

"Holy Mary, mother of God, pray for us sinners,
now and at the hour of our death. Amen."

Gospel: John 2:1-11